Finish Your Ark Now:

the Prudent Prepper's Primer!

By: JJ Noah © 2023 Emergency Health Enterprises, LLC

This book would not have been possible without the input of Mrs. Noah (especially on the Common Medical Issues and Provisioner sections). Thanks also to the many editors (you know who you are) who gave freely of their time and expertise!

I0202226

*Transportation options in tough times

*Making fuel, warmth and cooking

*Clothing needs

*Bush-crafting & snow caves

*Portable shelter options

*Factors to consider in deciding to move for safety

*Rural land – things you would need to know

*Methods to purify water

*Waste management

*Personal hygiene

*HAM radio and other communication options

*How to improve functional physical fitness

*Achieve body composition goals

*The mind, will and emotions

*Extreme stress management

*Faith vs. fear

*Understanding the spirit of man

*The importance of Hope

*Prospect of death without fear

*Prepare in this season for the coming season

*Your decision for personal responsibility

Finish Your Ark Now: the Prudent Prepper's Primer!

By: JJ Noah   © 2023 Emergency Health Enterprises, LLC

Introduction: The hardest part of any project is simply getting started! For you, that will mean actually reading this pocket book and picking one thing to physically accomplish for your first application. It is both smart and important to know what to do - saving time, money and emotional energy. These application steps are your "money-in-the-bank" when you need that all important withdrawal. The applications are divided up into specific areas to cover all of your bases when others will face extreme anxiety, do without, or even be taken under.

So, what if I never need any of this? Then count yourself lucky that you never needed to collect on your "insurance policy." Sleep soundly, while others worry and wish they had listened and prepared. It is often said "better early than one day late!" Proverbs 22:3 says "A prudent man foresees evil (danger) and hides himself, but the simple pass on and are punished" (suffer consequences). Maybe you are thinking that God alone (without involving you) will supernaturally take care of you daily until any crisis is over. Therefore, do you even need to prepare?

From the Bible stories of Noah ("by faith Noah... built an ark..." – Hebrews 11:7), we see that God used Noah's physical actions to preserve the human race as well as the animal kingdom. Joseph interpreted God's plan for the future <u>and then</u> physically stored up grain to feed his country of Egypt (and literally the known world) in time of extreme famine. From both of these Biblical accounts we learn that <u>preparation is the action of faith!</u> In the same way, for your present generation, you are to "...weigh carefully (judge) the words spoken..." (1 Corinthians 14:29) as penned in our day by JJ Noah.

Chapter 1: Why You Must Prepare Now

This book is one that I have been prepared to write as the result of a lifetime of experience and wisdom (yes, I am fully gray headed). While you may appreciate that I had to develop expertise in a multitude of areas to write credibly, please don't use us (my wife and I) as the standard for comparisons to your needed preparations. Instead, reason out (and ask God to lead you) in what you should do in your own situation. Understand that any value I bring is simply being a conduit of what God speaks for those who will hear - Jeremiah 1:9. (Note that all scripture is from the NKJV Bible and of course used with permission of the publisher – Thomas Nelson).

It is a timely message, for the short preparation period in which we now live and for the next season of chaos that is coming. It is simply a fact that we must prepare in this season for the next season – we can't wait or it will be too late! No other book I have found will teach and help prepare you physically, mentally, emotionally, and spiritually for this coming season. My goal is to distill many complex and interconnected matters into understandable and actionable plans.

I will lay out the case that the coming season of chaos is unlike what most of us have ever seen or imagined (even on TV). If I am wrong, and it is not really that bad, then you will be prepared for any number of likely lifetime occurrences such as: tornado (1,200 annually in the USA – more than the rest of the world combined), hurricane, flood, earthquake, massive wildfire, pestilence (think COVID, Spanish flu), famine (or just spiraling food costs), supply chain extended interruptions or shortages, riots, war, extended loss of electrical power, and you can complete this list for yourself.

So why do we think that things will not continue as they have these past years? Let's start with current reported news. The publication Foreignpolicy.com (1/28/21 report) says that corruption in the USA is the worst in a decade. Do you see our politicians acting in the best interests of the USA in fiscal responsibility, energy policies, border and national security, etc.? Then consider the government overreach of your freedoms associated with COVID, and the expectation of future serious COVID variants. The Pew Research Center (11/11/20 report) relays that in 2007-2017 there was a tremendous increase in religious persecution worldwide from both governmental and social forces (for example, 145 of the 198 countries persecute Christians). The Opendoors.org website reports that in 2022 at least 5,898 Christians were martyred, while over 6,175 were forcibly detained and 5,110 churches were attacked. We know that many other religions also are facing increased persecution and intolerance.

What about plans for a globalist New World Order (NOW) – eventually under a single ruling body (dystopian oligarchy)? These finalized events and its frightening consequences are recorded in the Bible books of Daniel and Revelation. The Georgia Guidestones are purported to be the NOW "ten commandments" and the first listed item is to "Maintain humanity under 500,000". Since the current world population is eight billion that is one enormous die-off that demands preparation to survive.

The USA has been fighting the War on Terror since 9/11 (2001). Iran, who is a future nuclear threat, calls the USA the "Great Satan", while their openly avowed mortal enemy Israel is only called the "Little Satan". Dr. Barbara Walter, a political scientist (University of California - San Diego) wrote the book *How Civil Wars Start: And How to Stop Them*. She says predictive factors of civil war are: countries waffling in the unstable zone between democracy and autocracy (sound familiar?) and also divided by identities of race (BLM, AIM, White Supremacists, etc.), ethnicity or religion. We know that armed militia groups from various fringe organizations within the country, as well as sleeper cell terrorists, are only awaiting orders and opportunity. The USA's Secretary of Energy admits that our nation's power grid is very vulnerable to terrorist attack. (Electricity is the lifeblood of the economy, fuel production, water pumping and the comforts of life).

Do you know that China and Russia have never renounced their goal of forcible world domination for communism? According to the International Monetary Fund (IMF), China is the world's largest creditor nation (owed $1.8 trillion), and the USA is now the world's largest debtor nation (owes $2.5 trillion). If the USA government were to default, would China and a coalition of nations (certainly Russia and possibly some Middle Eastern nations) come here to physically collect on cattle, gold reserves and other resources? China's active duty and paramilitary forces (2.2 million plus .5 million) is twice the USA active duty force (1.3 million) even before the addition of foreign cohort armies. A surprise attack with multiple fronts would overwhelm present USA military resources that have been downscaled. China's current military doctrine of "systems destruction warfare" - to destroy vital infrastructure is particularly worrisome in negating the USA force multiplier technologies.

At the very least, in a currency default, the USA would lose its position as the world's reserve currency (lose its ability to simply print dollars that are currently accepted in world trade). The USA is technically broke, yet spends over $50 billion annually in foreign aid, and additionally owes its own citizens obligations it can't continue to pay (Social Security, Medicare, etc.). What draconian steps might our government take to keep this sinking Titanic afloat for yet a while longer?

Finally, the weather and other geophysical events cost the USA $95 million in 2020 and affected one in three Americans. The Ecological Threat Register's 2020 report additionally showed a <u>10-fold increase</u> in these major events since 1960 (39 vs. 396 in 2019)! If you think of the present natural world as a safe place without colossal catastrophes, then look at the past with *Great Disasters: Dramatic True Stories of Nature's Awesome Power* published by Reader's Digest. So what disturbing news do you read about that we haven't mentioned?

Second, consider the words of some with a proven track record, that claim a knowing in their gut (physiologically, the gut and heart are actually connected to the brain by the vagus nerve). Some claim that God speaks to them in this way with words of knowledge - knowing what they could not otherwise know, words of wisdom - knowing what to do in that given situation and prophecy - foretelling future events. One of these men was the late John Paul Jackson who predicted (a word from the Lord in 2008) a coming "perfect storm." <u>Be sure and watch</u> his very important message "The Coming Perfect Storm" (on You-Tube) to decide for yourself.

Jackson said that five elements would converge to cause great upheaval in our entire world (and perhaps especially in the USA). These elements are 1) Political – poor policies and corruption; 2) Religious Conflicts – radical intolerance and persecution; 3) Wars – civil and worldwide; 4) Economic - upheavals and ultimately collapse; 5) Natural Disasters – both increased magnitude and numbers of geo-physical events.

Note that the sum of these elements is magnified/multiplied over what each element could do as individual parts. Also, that any one of these elements would be bad by itself, but Jackson says they will come in combined waves and then be repeated in varied combinations. A word picture to describe these five elements would be five sticks of dynamite placed against the wall of "Fortress America." ("Fortress America" is a term from the WW2 era that was used to describe the supposed invincibility of the USA borders). What is different now, as compared to the past, is that the fuse on these five elements has been lit and the devastating explosion is sure to follow!

Maybe you are not so sure of a modern day prophet - then what do you do with the vision that George Washington received at Valley Forge in 1777? The Library of Congress has this document of Washington's vision of the three great perils that would face the USA. Washington understood the first great peril to be the Revolutionary War and we certainly see the second great peril to be the Civil War between the states. We will therefore only examine the third great peril, predicted on American soil, which has yet to be fulfilled!

"Again I heard the mysterious voice saying, 'Son of the Republic look and learn.' At this the dark, shadowy angel placed a trumpet to his mouth, and blew three distinct blasts; and taking water from the ocean, he sprinkled it upon Europe, Asia and Africa. Then my eyes beheld a fearful scene. From each of these continents arose thick black clouds that were soon joined into one. And throughout this mass there gleamed a dark red light by which I saw hordes of armed men. These men, moving with the cloud, marched by land and sailed by sea to America, which country was enveloped in the volume of cloud. And I

dimly saw these vast armies devastate the whole country and the villages, towns and cities which I had seen springing up."

"As my ears listened to the thundering of the cannon, clashing of the swords, and the shouts and cries of millions in mortal combat, I again heard the mysterious voice saying, 'Son of the Republic, look and learn.' Where the voice had ceased, the dark shadowy angel placed his trumpet once more to his mouth, and blew a long and fearful blast."

"Instantly a light as of a thousand suns shone down from above me and pierced and broke into fragments the dark cloud which enveloped America. At the same moment the angel upon whose head still shown the word UNION, and who bore our national flag in one hand, and a sword in the other, descended from the heavens attended by legions of white spirits. These immediately joined the inhabitants of America, who I perceived were well-nigh overcome, but who immediately taking courage again, closed up their broken ranks and renewed the battle."

"Again, amid the fearful noise of the conflict I heard the mysterious voice saying, 'Son of the Republic, look and learn.' As the voice ceased the shadowy angel for the last time dipped water from the ocean and sprinkled it upon America. Instantly the dark cloud rolled back, together with the armies it had brought, leaving the inhabitants of the land victorious."

Louis Pasteur said "luck favors the prepared" – so Prepare Now! What about a prolonged disaster and/or a time of significant societal upheaval that you have already seen? Hurricane Katrina cost over $100-billion and took the Army Corps over 40-days just to pump out the water! The police were soon home protecting their own families while crime was rampant. Rebuilding has taken many years beyond the event. Also consider the initial as well as long term disruptions of COVID. Consider if the next pandemic could be even more frightening with immediate and serious side affects such as previously seen in the Black Plague or Ebola outbreaks.

<u>It is imperative that you use the last of the brief season that we are presently in to prepare for the next season of disruption and chaos.</u> Finish your "preparation ark" now – the flood is coming! Some may say, "Why would we even want to endure through all this?" In the final

chapter, I will reveal the future hope that can answer that question, but you have to survive the coming season in order to see it.

Chapter 2: The 5 Gs of Preparedness

Let's start with a true present day example. You come home to your place, in the middle of a winter snow or ice storm, which is now without electricity and perhaps even your phone doesn't seem to work. I have been there more than once – sometimes for less than a day and sometimes for several days. I have also spent many days and cold nights in the Rocky Mountains, in even more rugged situations, learning how to successfully adapt. Fortunately, I was trained as an Eagle Scout and practiced the Boy Scout motto of "be prepared!"

What you will need to remember is the 5 Gs of preparedness. Your immediate and first need is GEAR (physical stuff). Seeing at night is good - so you would need a flashlight with fresh batteries, maybe even a candle and matches. Staying warm is also good – so you need a heavy coat with wool hat and mittens, and a warm sleeping bag or blankets. Perhaps a battery operated radio would be helpful to find out why this is even happening in your area. For this night you decide to stay here, but other times you may need to leave home.

GEAR in a more extended crisis is best kept in a personal "bug-out" or "bug-in" pack or bag – just in case you needed to quickly leave your home for some reason. It is preloaded with all your necessities to last for several days (even if you stay in your home). The list of my packed items is provided in the A appendix: GEAR – "bug-out or "bug-in" pack or bag. Hopefully you have many of these items already that you just need to pull together (see Appendix B: Preparedness Quick Start). We also have a C Appendix: GEAR – Home or Small Group. These items tend to be less portable and can benefit not only you, but also your small support group in a more extended crisis. You may think of survival or comfort items that I have overlooked, so use your brain too.

If this list seems daunting then prioritize and do what you can (see Appendix D: Prep on a Budget). What if I (or my "Tribe" – small local support group) want/need only a few of these items for whatever reason? A Marine officer once told me 'make do, do without or innovate!' I would concur and also add "pray". James 4:2-3 says "....You fight and war Yet <u>you do not have because you do not ask.</u> ³ You ask and do not receive, because you ask amiss, that you may spend *it* on your pleasures." And finally the good word of Isaiah 30: 21 "Your ears shall hear a word behind you, saying, 'This *is* the way, walk in it,' "Whenever you turn to the right hand Or whenever you turn to the left."

Back to our present scenario, you wake up to find your situation has not changed, and so you need the second G of <u>GRUB (food and water)</u>. You have some bottled water, canned fruit, and beef jerky, etc. on-hand to get the calories you need to work. In an alternate scenario, do you remember the COVID quarantine where you were strongly encouraged not to go out? Many grocery stores were closed, others restricted buying quantities, and even then shelves were totally cleared out in just 3-days. Having adequate food and water at home takes you out of this uncomfortable situation. Eat what you Store and Store what you eat (keep it rotated so that first in is first out). See Appendix E: Food Storage list, which categorizes all types of food storage options.

Pick any combination(s) that you want based on food preferences, budget and storage space (cool and dark is best). Creative storage may be in a pantry, closet, crawl space, kitchen shelves/cabinets (or other living quarter shelves/cabinets), under beds, under stairs, in a storage building, basement or cellar, etc. Consider a storage tub to keep out mice and insects (set traps if needed and/or have a mouser cat). Tubs also help with water drips, but how do you keep out teens?

The government says an average calorie need for a day is 2,000 calories, but this need can be either more or less based on physical work requirements, age, body size and weight, pregnancy, etc. If you are considering buying pre-packaged meals (buckets or boxes) make sure the daily meal count for calories is not a fraction of 2,000 calories for price comparison. Also, look at the amount of protein and complex carbohydrates versus simple carbs (sugars) and fats. Consider the time that various food types can be stored without spoiling in your comparisons.

Getting a healthy and balanced diet is difficult if you aren't able to supplement these foods with fresh grown (Master-gardener needed). Vitamins are controversial and a complex science, but play the odds and consider having a basic multi-vitamin in your storage during the chaos season. Water can be stored in purchased bottles, but also self stored in liter bottles after soda or fruit juice. Plastic drum barrels (new or previously held non-toxic fluids like iodine, chlorine, etc.) that are thoroughly rinsed can hold water for washing and are probably drinkable as well.

The final question that always surfaces is how much Grub will you need to store? Enough food for you and your Tribe until other food sources are available (grocery stores are restocked, your Master-gardener crop is harvested or you secure a steady supply of game and/or fish). When the Israelites left the slavery of Egypt, and entered the wilderness to follow God, they carried food and water with them (preparation). When those prepared stores ran out <u>then God miraculously provided</u> water and manna (food). In case you are wondering, in the natural world, you can live three days without water and three weeks (or more) without food.

Having food to share with family, friends and neighbors is wonderful in normal times, but you really need to get them to prepare themselves for chaos times – so <u>get them this book!</u> Abe Lincoln said "You cannot help people permanently by doing for them, what they could and should do for themselves." Also, you don't want to be seen as the substitute for the God that they really need. Using the WW2 slogan - "Loose lips sink ships" – you don't want hungry observers to think of your house as a free grocery.

Does Jesus teach that you are obligated to share in all situations? Matthew 25:1-13 is a parable (teaching story) that Jesus told about five wise virgins and five foolish virgins (virgins signify that they are all good people vs. bad people). The five wise have oil enough to perform their duties, but the foolish have not adequately prepared and run out of oil. The foolish beg for oil, but are told to go and buy their own oil in town (late night), and as a result they miss out (are excluded) from the wedding feast. The foolish are chided in this teaching story and the wise are never condemned for not sharing and then coming up short themselves.

Therefore, your preparation priorities must be decided by you, but consider: yourself, dependant family and your Tribe first. Perhaps all you can do for most of the others you care about – close friends, adult family, extended family, church, school, work place colleagues, your neighborhood and others in your community is to <u>urge them to prepare now, and give them a copy of this pocket book</u>, because you simply can't physically help everyone! Note that it is <u>not</u> your goal to create fear, but to encourage faith (and <u>preparation is the action of faith</u>)!

If this present story continues for a several days, you will need the third G: <u>GREENBACKS</u> (I could have said Gold, but that would of course not be politically correct). You are eventually going to run out of supplies that need to be purchased or bartered for in trade. What about your credit cards? If the power is out, your cards can purchase nothing (been there, and it's not pleasant). A local merchant that knows you may take a check, but cash should be good or you can barter. Therefore, it is always wise to carry some cash in small bills.

In a longer term crisis, such as a "banking holiday/disruption" or if the credit market dries up (credit is not being extended to people or businesses) then you may need greenbacks to buy the things you need and want. Signs are sometimes posted at businesses that they won't take bills larger than a $20. Therefore, your bills should be in $5, $10 and $20 dollar denominations. In this case, cash will be king (people will want your cash), but if the government declares bankruptcy then no one will accept these now declared worthless dollars.

What is perceived as a monetary equivalent could be "money-metal" or gold and silver. These are also a store of value (keep their same buying power) in times of high inflation – when it takes more dollars to buy the same amount of goods. Historically gold is probably at least ten times the value of silver (or more). You might want fractional (1/2 ounce, ¼ ounce) gold coins for smaller items, but there aren't a lot of these out there. Silver fills this niche and comes as a bar (beware - larger bars could be filled with lead) or 1 ounce rounds (coin shape-size). "Junk silver" is 1964 and older USA coins (half-dollars, quarters and dimes) that are 90% silver content. They have circulated as money in previous days and therefore should be accepted once again.

Coin dealers might try and sell you "numismatic coins" which sell for a premium based on their value to coin collectors. This is a very volatile market (just like art and antiques) and the ease to convert to cash is much more difficult or even impractical. Diamonds and other precious jewels are also less liquid, but can be a big store of value in a tiny or hidden space. Bullets often served as small change (if you don't have pocket change) in other modern countries during collapsed economies. Other barter items, generally accepted in trade include coffee, alcohol, chocolate, cigarettes, tobacco (anything addictive), lighters, candles, batteries, chlorine dioxide water purification tablets, duct tape and of course TP, etc.

It is said that "even good men do bad things in desperate situations." This leads us to the fourth G: <u>GUARD-DOG</u> (you perhaps thought I was going to say Guns, but once again that would be the very politically incorrect alternative). Most dogs are noise makers, and thieves don't like noise. Even a recording of a dog barking may be enough to scare them away. Even small dogs that aren't trained to attack still have teeth and can bite (the germs in their mouth may be worse than their bite). Some breeds of dogs, such as German Shepherds, are routinely used by both police and the military with attack training. Our German Shepherd was a family pet and never trained to attack, but leaped over a couch when our daughter's friend surprisingly grabbed her and she squealed. We have no doubt that she would have been rescued.

You could choose to share, but criminals often aren't big on sharing, and may just take it all! I am charged to protect my family and perhaps you feel the same way? Maybe you can successfully subdue a thief/rapist/criminal with non-lethal force, but as was illustrated in an

Indiana Jones movie – don't just take a sword to a gun fight. Therefore, we will now discuss guns.

When my daughter first graduated from graduate school she was working into the evening hours and had to go to the parking lot alone. If you are in this situation, see if there is anyone that can escort you to your car at the very least (and probably have a flashlight that can also serve as a baton). I taught a college course on self defense for women and many of them attended after a close encounter with bad guys (motivation). Most of the time, they related situations that should have been avoided in the first place. Examples included: someone jumped in my car when I stopped at a traffic light (my doors were not locked); someone grabbed my arm and pulled me along (it was at night, in front of a bar, in a bad part of town – and you were there why?); you get the idea.

My class taught situational awareness and watchful vigilance, how not to look like an easy target, not taking stupid chances or being in risky situations, how to break grabs and holds, kicks and punches in vital target spots, etc. Classes like this are available, or at the very least watch You-Tube (and practice). Equipment for sparring (light contact fight training) includes mouth guards, cups (for males), and contact padding. Perhaps someone in your Tribe has some knowledge and experience that can help train others who are interested in developing these skills. Heavy punching bags (50-100 pounds - garage sale item) can be used for self defense training (kicks, punches, etc.) at home.

Back to my daughter, she said "I want something to stop a bad guy, but I don't want to hurt them". If a moral compass and the law don't deter bad behavior, then physical force and pain are your only alternatives (if police can't come fast enough). Non-lethal weapons include: pepper-spray, and pepper ball firearms, "flash-bang" grenades (civilian versions are generally legal), stun-guns, sling-shot (with a wrist brace these can pack a wallop), a club (baton, baseball bat), rubber bullets or rock salt (specialty shot-gun loads). Potentially lethal weapons if you just don't want a gun - include: bladed weapons (knife, throwing knifes or ninja stars, sword, spear, etc.), bow and arrows or

15

cross-bow with ammo bolts. Note that all of these will require practice to be proficient and an appropriate backstop for safety.

If you are ready to consider a GUN then I personally recommend economical practice with a BB or pellet gun (comes in both rifle and pistol options; which is how I teach grandkids). Practice plinking cans or shooting targets in the forest, desert, your back yard and even your basement or garage (special backstop catchers can be made or purchased). After this training it is time to get some ear plugs and ear muffs for regular firearms. Rent (try before you buy) or purchase a .22 caliber rifle or pistol (has light recoil and not overly loud) and do get some professional instruction at this point.

Rifles in order of simplicity of design come in bolt action, lever action, pump action and semi-automatic (pull the trigger and a new shell is automatically inserted each time). Pistols in the same ranking order are commonly single shot (think old west little derringers), single action revolvers (think cowboy pistols that must have the hammer pulled back by the thumb before the trigger can be pulled), double action revolvers (longer trigger pull to rotate the 6-bullet (generally) cylinder into firing position, but then fires with a trigger pull) and semi-automatic (new shell is put in the firing chamber automatically with each trigger pull.

There is also a .22 WMR (.22 Magnum) pistol and rifle that is one-third more powerful than a regular .22, but its ammo is about three times as expensive. The .22 magnum shells are longer and slightly wider which means that this ammunition is _not_ interchangeable with regular .22 firearms. Ammo for a .22 or .22 magnum generally comes in a 50-round box. We have seen multiple times when ammo of any kind is simply not available, so keep at least a hundred bullets on hand at all times. Hollow point shells (of any caliber) tend to create larger and more damaging wounds. (Hollow point shells are identified on the box and by the hole in the center of the bullet's nose).

The best home defense gun is arguably a shorter barrel shotgun (these are legally purchased). Lightest kick is a .410-guage, then a 20-gauge and finally a 12-guage which has the biggest kick and most stopping power. Shotguns come in a brake barrel (to load the shell) single shot or double barrel (like the old west movies), pump loaded or semi-automatic. Purchase special shotgun shells with .00-buck shot (just like the sheriff used in old western movies) – simply point and shoot a wide hole. These shells will probably come in a 5 pack. Birdshot loads (tiny bb pellets) are not as effective for self defense, but come in a box of 20 shells and are considerably cheaper for practice.

Shotguns are designed for hunting ducks, geese, pheasants and other birds (good fresh meat). When considering higher caliber guns then think about the common availability of ammunition. My adult Tribe all have .22's or shotguns (we can hunt rabbits and fowl), but we also try and have as much overlap as possible in any other ammunition calibers (to share bullets).

The most common military/police calibers in use are probably a 9-millimeter semi-automatic hand gun and a .223 caliber semi-automatic rifle. These are not auto-fire machine guns, but will fire a bullet each time the trigger is pulled. Both of these are probably magazine fed (bullets are loaded into a rectangular metal magazine) and then the magazine inserts into the weapon. An alternative to an external magazine for holding the bullets is an internal magazine (such as a tube that is part of the rifle). WW2 era rifles may have a clip (metal strip that holds the bullets together – see pictures on You-Tube).

Multiple magazines can be carried in a vest, pouch or pocket. Depending on the mission, the military may carry at least 4 - 8 magazines. The advantage of having bullets in a magazine (vs. a box) is that they are ready to quickly fire. External magazine sizes (the number of bullets they carry) can range from 3 – 100 shells depending on the caliber of bullet, but magazine size may be regulated by law. Extreme nervousness makes it harder to do the precise finger motions required to get bullets into a magazine. Think of trying to do a precise fingering movement in the cold or with gloves/mittens. There are simple devices (magazine loaders) to help quickly load a magazine with ammunition that are very helpful – so get these for your firearms.

Firearms are not cheap (even used), but the money you will spend on ammunition will probably be the greater expense (if not a .22 or shotgun shell choice). Ammo can be reloaded, if you save the shell casing, but this takes special equipment, bullet parts and gunpowder (maybe a trade with another Tribe?). You may also need a holster for a pistol carry (many choices to fit your gun size) and a sling for a rifle.

For concealed carry you will need a permit, some States allow open carry (pistol showing), some cities ban any and all handguns (check local laws). Common pistol calibers are .380 (if a 9MM is too much kick), 38-special (what cops carried in the Andy Griffith days), .45 caliber (army sidearm WW2), 357 magnum (mountain bear protection) and 44 magnum (Grizzly bear protection and "Dirty Harry's" carry).

Hunting rifles and the rifles military snipers use have a larger caliber bullet (308, 30-30, 30-06, 303-Winchester, etc.) with a bigger shell casing and more gun powder (more recoil to the shooter). The means of loading the bullet into these rifle chambers are commonly bolt action, lever action and the semi-automatic previously discussed. These firearms often have a scope to better see the target (magnification and size of view). The downside of scopes, besides their cost, is that they are fragile (bumps, etc. can throw off their sight alignment).

Firearms come with iron sights, so you don't have to purchase additional optics. However, there are other firearm sights that are available in the following price order. Fiber optic sights are simple pieces of plastic that illuminate (appear to glow) with sunlight. Night sights appear to glow in the dark (luminous paint without batteries like a watch). Laser sights project a dot (red laser maybe 10-yards; green laser maybe 25-yards) on a close range target. They are battery operated and have an off/on switch. Finally, a micro red-dot sight allows you to put a dot on a target (works well at night) and shoot with both eyes open. It is battery powered (good battery life) and always stays on. Probably what you won't have because of cost is thermal imaging and true night vision (what you might see on TV). What you should get, at relatively low cost, is a pair of binoculars or maybe even a spotting scope (see shots fired in training).

If you watch news footage of our military troops, you will see that most carry a pistol on their hip as well as a rifle. This gives them a back-up in case of firearm malfunction or the need to reload a magazine and still be able to quickly return fire. They will also carry a knife for close quarter defense. Go to the range and practice frequently - also learn how to clean the weapon (dirty weapons can jam-up, so you will need a gun cleaning kit for daily use). Some folks purchase (or make from a kit) black powder rifles or pistols (think single shot revolutionary war musket) because they believe these would never be outlawed?

Decide where you will store and/or place your firearms to keep them safe from children, but yet be accessible in a defense situation (this is not an easy choice). There are gun safes and locking storage cabinets, as well as individual firearm trigger locks (see what your local laws are). It is generally recommended that ammunition be stored separately from the firearm, or at the very least that a bullet not be in the firing chamber. These are very tough decisions and there are lots of factors that may be unique for your own home situation. Final bit of advice is don't ever draw a gun unless you are willing to use it - or it may be used against you!

The scriptural basis for the use of potentially deadly force is outlined in the Protector section (please read). If you use any weapon in self defense will you feel guilt? Most would say that you probably will feel guilt (maybe false guilt), but what does the Bible say about this subject? One of the ten-commandments is "Thou shalt not kill" (more accurately translated as "Thou shalt not murder" – you do know the difference right?). Exodus 22:2 says "If the thief is found breaking in, and he is struck so that he dies, *there shall be* no guilt for his bloodshed."

Perhaps you have the first four Gs covered: GEAR, GRUB, GREENBACKS and GUARD-DOG, but do you have the fifth G of <u>GOD</u>? Why is GOD relevant in preparedness? Because when you have done everything in <u>your power</u> you are probably still short on something! Well doesn't God take care of everyone? He could, but Psalm 91:14 - 16 explains that truly <u>counting on God's care is based on genuine</u>

<u>mutual relationship</u>. Verse 14 says: "Because YOU love me" says the Lord, "I will rescue YOU and protect YOU for YOU know my Name". This is not a casual acknowledgement, but a covenant relationship (think good marriage, but more detail on this later). Verse 15 says: "YOU will call upon me, and I will answer YOU; I will be with YOU in trouble, I will deliver YOU and honor YOU". Verse 16 says: "With a long life I will satisfy YOU and show YOU my salvation" (present life and after-life). Psalm 34:7 provides us with further insight into this relationship with God. It says: "The angel of the Lord encamps around those who fear <u>(reverence) Him</u>, and He delivers..." – non inclusive list.

Out of the 5 Gs, perhaps the GOD-relationship should be the first G, but I suspect that you wanted to think that you were totally responsible for your own preparedness and success. In time, you might even come to believe like I do, that all that I have, all that I am, and all that I ever hope to be rests in the Lord. It is an unequal partnership - I can't do it without Him and He won't do it without me (yes, you are still responsible for the first four Gs). Maybe you think you are so prepared and your core skills are so good that you don't need God. Perhaps God's answer to you then is found in Proverbs 16:18, "Pride goes before destruction, a haughty spirit before a fall." Solomon (the wisest man who ever lived) penned these words under God's anointing – so who am I to dispute them? The famous Christian author C.S. Lewis advises: "Christianity if false is of no importance, and if it is true, of infinite importance. The only thing it can't be is moderately important."

God gave Moses the 10 commandments (not the 10 suggestions). "If you love Me, you will keep My commandments" (John 14:15). Jesus is presented as "savior" 13 times in the Bible, but as "Lord" (absolute boss) over 700 times. Know that you cannot expect the long-term blessings of God without the God of the blessing (lived out in obedient discipleship). "My sheep hear My voice, and I know them, and they follow Me. [28] And I give them eternal life, and they shall never perish; neither shall anyone snatch them out of My hand" (John 10:27-28). Additionally, Proverbs 14:32 says: "There is a way that seems right to a man, But its end is the way of death." Alternatively, to learn the way of life – read on in Appendix F: GOD-relationship.

Chapter 3: Skills That Increase Your Survivability & Service to Others

In our example of a power-down winter experience at home, or perhaps your car breaks down in the country, what are the basic skills that might be needed? The first four Gs dealt with stuff: GEAR stuff, GRUBB stuff, GREENBACK (plus) stuff and GUARD-DOG (plus) stuff. All things that I can purchase if I know what to get (see the appendices for lists). The fifth G of GOD is relational help and something that you develop (see its appendix to better understand how this actually works and why it is so important). While the G stuff and God are extremely important, you also need to develop skills and abilities to help both yourself and others.

Basic self-reliance skills I learned as an Eagle Scout, and later refined on my own, could include the following list: how do you dress in layers for warmth, start a fire (two matches and no gas), establish a shelter, purify water for drinking, tie rope knots, find food and cook over an open fire, read a map and basic orienteering/navigation to start the list. Maybe you think you will never need these skills - and perhaps you are right - but what are the consequences if you are wrong? Others may have learned these skills previously in the Scouts, military or from friends and family. Perhaps you are saying "I missed this stage of skill development" (my adopted sister grew up in a huge eastern metropolis and never even saw the countryside/wilderness before meeting our Rocky Mountain family). It is not too late to learn, and you can pay for a course to teach you, find friends that will teach you, join a group that does camping or learn the skills on You-Tube (but you still have to actually practice these skills to be proficient!).

You would probably say that you have developed your vocational skills so that are really good at the particular job you do (and make a good living). However, in the Great Depression, many competent people lost their jobs (for a season) or had their wages drastically reduced. Most decreased their expenses by what they could learn to do for themselves or simply did without. I consider myself to be really good at my professional job and yet one big company I worked for went bankrupt. I was laid off in another job (fortune 50 company) when their current workforce was cut by 20% in a single day. Career skills are important as they can get you back to traditional work faster.

Understanding the need for a Tribe

In a longer-term crisis, the core skills needed to survive and even thrive can be encapsulated into eight "core job skill descriptions". While I personally try and develop as many of these skills as possible, I know that I am personally deficient in some areas. The Lone Ranger found he could start to fix this by having Tonto as a partner (loners will get picked off). In real life, a "Tribe" or small group of people (this could be my family or a small group of select friends that live close) cover my deficiencies and supplement my areas of strength.

In practicality, the size of a Tribe is limited by the number of people you can feed. This mutual help provides synergy – where the total effect is greater than the sum of its parts. The Clydesdale horse analogy illustrates this principle marvelously. While a single horse can pull 7,000 pounds – two horses together can pull 18,000 pounds; but if they are properly matched and trained they can pull 25,000 pounds (the equivalent of a full extra horse).

My "4 Ms and 4 Ps" list of core skill set groups is as follows: 1) Master-gardener; 2) Medical; 3) Mechanic; 4) Merchant; 5) Protector; 6) Provisioner; 7) Priest; 8) Pre-crisis job skills. We will examine each of these core skill sets starting with Master-gardener (note that we say Master-gardener versus a cursory gardening knowledge). There is a lot to know about growing food, fighting pests and weeds, harvesting and preserving food, saving seed and care of animals. Once you eat all your stored food, how do you plan to get more?

Perhaps you live in an area where there is enough fish, game and foraging (assuming that you have the basic skills) to supply all of your nutritional needs. Most of us at best, can only hope to supplement our diet in this way. Growing vegetables, maybe fruit and perhaps some animal husbandry (think chickens for eggs or maybe meat rabbits) is a more likely bet for the majority of us. Don't panic over this concept, as someone else in your Tribe has this niche covered (or recruit that someone). Remember - the size of your Tribe is at least limited to how many mouths you can feed.

So what are your chances of having a farm or ranch family in your Tribe? Less than 2% of the US population is farm or ranch families. Your next question should be what if I have some knowledge and experience, but don't even have my own yard, so how can I have a "Victory Garden" (WW2 reference)? You may still be able to grow some plants in shallow soil pots – what you need is seeds, soil, sunlight and water. Food herbs that you can grow in small places include: cilantro, lemon grass, thyme, basil and tarragon. Three medicinal herbs that you can grow easily are Roman chamomile, mint and Aloe-Vera. Fruits and vegetables to grow in an apartment include: peppers, bush beans on a trellis, salad greens, green onion, cherry tomatoes and strawberries. Consider sprouting seeds for food with a Mason jar and mesh sprouting lid (complete sprouting kits can be purchased) or get the details from a You-Tube video. Sprouting seeds gives you more food volume than the seed itself as well as additional nutrients.

If you have your own yard then you should consider putting in or really expanding on a garden. Chances are you will then need to purchase or make nutrient rich soil. Soil is not just dirt; it should also consist of organic matter (decaying plants and protein) and living organisms (bacteria and fungi), because live soil makes live food. You can purchase this soil or eventually compost it to make your own soil (You-Tube video for sure). Composting uses soil - for bacteria, green matter (decaying plants, grass, leaves, coffee grounds, manure, etc.) for nitrogen and brown matter (wood chips, saw dust, ash, etc.) for carbon. Then it is a process of time with moisture, high temperature and oxygen to turn these elements into live soil.

After you secure a garden plot (maybe a raised bed or community plot) - even another yard (neighbor/friend's yard, etc.) then what do you grow? Six plants that are calorie dense for relatively small plots include: potatoes, sweet corn, pumpkin, cabbage (not calorie dense, but nutrient dense), tomatoes and beans. Seeds can be purchased in bulk from a seed company or you can get a vacuum sealed can with sealed pouches that could serve as a seed bank. Do <u>get seeds now!</u>

In the Rocky Mountain area we have a short growing season (adequate warmth and sunlight). You can find your area growing season on-line, at the local nursery or from a seed catalogue. Personally, we extend this season by starting to grow some seeds inside (grow lights are ideal) and then transition them outside. A "cold frame" structure is a wood box with a clear top up against the house. Alternatively, our plants could go to raised beds with hoops that are covered with "freeze cloth" (looks like a Conestoga wagon). We also constructed a three season Quonset hut (rebar hoop frame covered in plastic sheeting with roll up sides) that can help in early spring and late fall to extend the growing season.

We purchased a book called "MiniFARMING: Self Sufficiency on ¼ Acre" by Brett L. Markham (ISBN 978-1-60239-984-6). Some Rocky Mountain States with water restrictions allow a single acre to be irrigated with a domestic well. This assumes that you don't have water rights with an irrigation company or other water resources that you own. Living where it regularly rains negates this hassle for irrigation. Will the land need to be cleared for crops or can it be used as is for pasture grazing? Do you have an additional wooded area for hunting, wild crafting and wood gathering?

What if your Tribe wants to lease an even larger plot of ground or maybe you have a family farm that you are ready to live on (at least for this season of time). There are about two million farms in the US (250 million acres) and most every one of them does not have adequate labor for what will probably be needed. About half of the land in the US is agricultural grazing for animals. So let's take time out to discuss animals that you might be able to raise for food.

If you live in town with a large private yard, you might be able to raise rabbits (reproduce quickly and ready to butcher in 10-12 weeks at 5-6 pounds). Two doe and a buck may produce nearly 600 pounds of meat in a year (that's more meat than a one year old steer!). For this volume though, you would need to have 5-6 rabbit hutch shelters (build out of wire and wood scrap). Rabbit manure is not "hot" and so it can be added directly to your garden without composting (great benefit). Details can be found on the familyfarmlivestock.com website.

Chickens are increasingly acceptable in town as well – without the rooster of course! Chickens can be raised for eggs or for meat – check varieties for the best breeds of each type. Cornish cross chicks can be ready to butcher in only 6 weeks, while Heritage meat bird breeds are about 10 weeks to slaughter. Egg producers go from chicks to laying eggs in 18 weeks. They will need a chicken coop of some type and containment if you let them "free range" (fencing can be traditional or a portable solar fence).

We constructed a "chicken tractor" which is a big wooden box with roost bars inside (chickens like to sleep off the ground). The chicken tractor has a roof, wire sides and no bottom (so grass and bugs are exposed for the chickens to eat). Every couple of days you pull it forward for new grazing, while it keeps the chickens safe and contained (see plans and operation on You-Tube). Note that you are fertilizing the grass as a side benefit besides not mowing.

If you are in a more rural setting, you may be able to raise additional rabbits and chickens or you could expand to pigs, lambs/goats and cattle (any or all). Animals can be raised for milk, meat, hides, wool (made into yarns for textiles). Animals come in all sizes (think miniature cows) and vary in characteristics of how much milk they produce, etc. Dairy goats produce a lot of milk for a small animal, but are difficult to fence. A good local county extension agent can supplement your own research for informed selection.

When you are ready for meat you can learn to butcher your own or you can have it done for you. Chickens are pretty quick/easy to process and don't require specialized equipment. Larger animals (including big game) can be butchered with the simple tools of a boning knife, trimming knife and cleaver or hack saw for bones. We then put the meat pieces in saran-wrap and butcher paper or alternatively use a seal-a-meal vacuum to seal them for the freezer. Alternatively, meat can be smoked or made into jerky strips (sliced thin, heavily salted and dried) to preserve it without the need for refrigeration. There are techniques to be learned to turn fresh meat into quality dried meat.

What technically determines a ranch is growing livestock (beef, pork, lamb, etc.). Farms grow crops, but either one may do both (animals and crops). As a couple, we constructed a small farmstead – alfalfa (baled for dairy feed), organic raspberries (an easy to grow perennial crop, but laborious to pick) and various vegetables (grown in raised beds), orchard – apples and pears, but also have a few registered beef cattle (sold as breeding stock or the steers for beef) and chickens (egg production). Please note that we share this information for background reference only – you don't necessarily need to do what we have done! Perhaps, you have even decided that you have enough other needed core skills that you can mostly trade for your food?

There seems to be a mystique about orchards – lots of people think they want one. Apples and pears are perennial crops (come back on their own every year) and are nutrient dense good tasting calories. We also have some peach, apricot and plumbs, but they are more delicate. However, they all must be pruned heavily every year (takes some skill and lots of time), plus weeding and mowing. Orchards must be sprayed regularly (organic or not) for disease prevention and bugs. Picking is the easy part, but canning (apple sauce, pie filling and apple butter), drying apple chips, freezing apple slices in bags, etc. takes lots of time and many hands.

So what do all of these garden plots, farms and ranches have in common? Quite frankly – lots of opportunities (hard work)! The Garden of Eden is long gone and now we have horticulture (plants) and animal husbandry (breeding and care of animals). What we battle day in and day out are the 5 Ws: 1. Weather (especially wind, but also too hot and too cold); 2. Weevils (and other bug pests, sometimes reptile or mammal pests), 3. Water (too much rain or usually not enough – enter irrigation work), 4. Weeds (must be hand pulled, burned, sprayed, mechanically plowed under, scraped off, mowed and trimmed constantly); 5. Work (sometimes dawn till dusk)!

It is a great lifestyle (the views, mostly fresh air, a more independent and self sufficient lifestyle, sometimes working with family – young and old both can significantly contribute). However, it is also a tough lifestyle (long hours, low pay, no guarantee of the size of a crop, sometimes chemical sprays, inclement weather, and broken equipment). You need to know the pros and cons upfront, but you can do this if you need to (this is for a season, not forever unless you decide). One of the things that I remind myself of, in the boring tasks, is that my real boss is a Jewish carpenter. Colossians 3:23-24 says: "And whatever you do, do it heartily, as to the Lord and not to men, [24] knowing that from the Lord you will receive the reward of the inheritance; for you serve the Lord Christ."

For the overachiever, or the idealistic city dweller, a farm/ranch may seem like the ideal (forever) lifestyle change (and for some it may be). However, consider the present economic facts: 90% of farm family income is not made on the farm (seeking insurance and steady salary in-town). Farm commodity prices can have bad years, but the return even in good years tends not to be enough to really compensate and off-set expenses. Of course, all of this paradigm could shift positively in the coming season of chaos. Presently though, farm foreclosures are not uncommon and farm credit policies for family farms are tough (lots of costs upfront for seed and planting with an uncertain harvest months away), and there is no parity pricing (living wage scale).

On the flip side, most farm land itself appreciates over time and makes a profit when sold (think of farm land itself as a good investment). In the past, the US government held grain reserves to support farm commodity prices in bumper years (and as food insurance to feed people in lean years), but no more! One more thing to consider, if you have very little money after getting your Gear and Grub, is trading your labor to a farmer who needs the help. If you are new to production agriculture, there is a huge learning curve, so partnership with a farmer/rancher is well worth the trading of your time. Share cropping is an arrangement where the farmer supplies the land and some equipment and you supply the labor. Then you both share in the crop (maybe 50/50 on a small piece of ground?).

Alternatively, you/your Tribe must come up with the considerable infrastructure that progressively larger pieces of land require to make a harvest. Examples are fencing for animals (keep them in or out), shed structures for animals and for equipment, and tools, etc.). However, leasing land (and maybe even any existing equipment) may be a better decision for someone who needs their cash for operating expenses (buying livestock, animal feed, seed, etc.) and particularly if you only plan to be on the farm/ranch for the crisis period.

In most any gardening or farm operations you will need appropriate work clothes. Denim pants and shirt (maybe even a coverall for cold season), heavy socks, work boots (leather and also rubber boots for water/mud), full-brim sun hat, sun glasses, leather gloves and fabric gloves with rubbery grip palms. Think about what other kinds of tasks are required of a farmer/rancher or Master Gardener with the help of many hands from your Tribe?

The second core skill set is Medical, because Master Gardeners, hunters/fishers/gatherers and others will get sick or hurt. My wife and I know this from many years of personal experience, and we have the scars to prove it! The most basic medical need is first-aid for when injuries occur. Perhaps you have had or will consider doing in the very near future; basic first-aid training such as is offered through the Red Cross, Scouts or the military. We have provided item lists for various level med kits, and suggest some medical/first-aid reference books in Appendix H: Medical Items Kit Lists. Common Medical Conditions and Potential Treatments (Appendix I) is an outstanding concise reference, for even non-medically trained people, and covers the most frequent issues faced. (The true team authors are an ER Nurse and an EMR).

Perhaps your Tribe, like our Tribe, will have a professional level medical provider, or you need to understand who can best help you. The first professional level (state and national registry) of emergency care is an EMT (emergency medical technician) or alternatively an EMR (emergency medical responder). EMRs forgo the ambulance driving component and are working under their own doctor's written medical oversight. These certifications typically require a junior college level semester of training that includes both classroom and hands-on practical situations. A paramedic will perhaps have two years of training, and a registered nurse will typically have a four year college degree. PAs (Physician Assistants) and NPs (Nurse Practitioners) essentially have a master's degree (two years of graduate training) and can usually write prescriptions for drugs. Physicians or Medical Doctors have four years of graduate schooling, plus additional training as a resident and intern. Physicians can further specialize in various areas such as cardiology, neurology, orthopedics (bone/joint), etc. There are also several allied health personnel such as certified athletic trainers (C.AT), physical therapists (PT or DPT), chiropractors, etc. that should be competent in emergency medical situations.

Dentists, pharmacists, veterinarians, and numerous other health-professionals might be a part of your small Tribe, or more likely found in your local Community (friendly groups of Tribes in a geographic area that may trade skill set expertise). Finally, community disease prevention and sanitation will be an extremely important skill set for this group. Note: natural health (including herbs) and wellness is also important, but usually will not be taught within most traditional medical training models. Therefore, we will provide some appropriate information in these areas as well.

Invariably someone will ask "can I grow medicinal herbs if the pharmacy is not available"? The simple answer is YES, but there is a ton to learn – order seeds now (or identify plants in the wild – which is called wild-crafting). Growing herbs, preparing and using herbs (alcohol-tinctures, poultices, teas, vinegars, hot infusions, cold infusions, decoctions, infused oils, salves/balms, herbal pills and cream ointments is a tall order. You will also be purchasing eye-dropper brown bottles (protect it from sun) and other supplies. Therefore, survival medicinal use will require good herbal preparation books and someone to really read, study and understand them. Medicinal potions that are prepared and/or administered incorrectly might cause harm versus help.

I have attended some excellent on-line seminars led by Dr. Patrick Jones DVM, who is both a clinical herbalist and a veterinarian. Therefore, he can test his herbs on his animal patients first. He also sells the seeds (to grow your own plants) as well as pre-concocted herbal remedies ready for application. One of his books is *The Home Grown Herbalist* and he does run a School of Botanical Medicine if you desire to specialize in this craft and perhaps even one-day certify as a Clinical Herbalist (homegrownherbalist.net). My wife is more familiar with Amy Fewell who wrote The Homesteader's Herbal Companion and has many other products as well (thefewellhomestead.com). We also have a book – DK's Encyclopedia of Herbal Medicine: The Definitive Reference to 550 Herbs and Remedies for Common Ailments by Andrew Chevallier (www.dk.com).

One related skill that is fairly easy to do is to make your own <u>colloidal silver, a natural anti-biotic</u> that has been safely used for over a thousand years. Materials needed are three 9-volt batteries (or a 30-volt plug-in transformer), two 100% silver coins/bars (think new American Eagle 100% silver dollars vs. old 90% US silver dollars), two alligator clips with wires (one attaches to each silver bar/coin, and negative/positive to the batteries), distilled water, a plastic clip for holding the coins near each other in the water (but keeping the alligator clips out of the water) and a glass jar (yep – follow You-Tube instructions on set-up and processing). The bubbles on the coin will tell you that the process of transferring the silver ions to the water is working. The color of the water provides an estimate of the ionic concentration (Tyndall effect). Light yellow might be as low as 2ppm (parts per million) and dark yellow might be 20 ppm (typical of purchased colloidal silver). Actual measurement of the TDS (total dissolved solids) can be accomplished with a quality water tester. Place the finished product in a brown/amber glass jar to protect it from light and store in a cool place.

One example of a homegrown anti-biotic: our daughter takes the elder berries that we grow and cooks them (raw berries may be toxic) into a syrup with cloves, cinnamon, ginger and honey. This has been used for hundreds of years to boost the immune system and fight off cold and especially flu (use at first symptoms – 15 milliliters 3-5 times per day) according to Web MD (but of course check with your own healthcare provider).

The next core skill set is a Mechanic - because vital stuff breaks and needs to be repaired or new stuff needs to be designed and built. These folks may be gifted fabricators with various training experiences from alternative high schools, trade schools, or apprentice programs (including family training) up to engineering related degrees. While we have housed this skill set under the umbrella term Mechanic – this could include any of the skill trades (carpenters, welders, auto mechanics, electricians, plumbers, facility maintenance, blacksmiths, etc.). Nerdy college trained engineers, particularly when teamed up with a gifted fabricator can make some amazing stuff!

I am not a mechanic, but have learned some skills and experiences to allow me to be a support to those in my Tribe who are mechanics. I have learned to operate some heavy equipment (road building) and tractors with various equipment attachments (farming operations) and have assisted in building: some Habitat for Humanity houses (framing, drywall and roofing) as well as farm fences, irrigation (install and repair), various sheds and farm tool repair. I do have problem solving skills (developed from my "real job") that frequently serve as the basis for our Tribe to come up with refined designs to be fabricated.

I admire those with the talents and refined skills to fix what needs to be fixed or to build projects from scratch. If you serve your Tribe in this way then they are fortunate indeed to have you. Please consider those in your Tribe who you can mentor with your skills and to assist you. You will know what tools and equipment you will need in your specialties so I won't go there. However, the following is a list of tools that most Tribes should consider having (or perhaps already have) for routine maintenance. Appendix J: Mechanic Tools List is my personal list of tools for farm and house maintenance as a non-mechanic (your mechanic will probably request more)! Maybe you can get everything at an estate sale, or conversely pick up a starter tool box set and add from there.

Can you develop a library of books, You-Tube videos, on-line classes, etc. for rudimentary and reference training in many of these skills? One of my grandfathers was a Master Barn Builder and Master Machinist (one of my brothers hogged this gene), but also consider the core skill sets typically attributed to more self-reliant groups such as the Amish or Mennonite communities.

The Merchant is the next core skill-set that could be vital to you and/or your Tribe. The Merchant is the catchall term for procurement - the barterer, scrounger (think Radar O'Reilly in the M.A.S.H. TV series who made all the connections to get anything needed). This person might also be thought of as an entrepreneur or capitalist (perhaps even with present income or other savings resources). This skill set values the thrill of putting together a series of swaps that might seem impossible to others.

The Merchant probably handles most of the business affairs of the Tribe. If you grow it - they sell/trade your surplus for what you do need. For example, most Master-gardeners are really good at food production activities, but not so good at developing markets (guilty as charged). This is true despite the fact that one of my college degrees is in business management (yes - my Dad made me study this subject).

Marketing and social media are now inseparable. It is important that you have contacts for all the things that you might need to trade for in the future. The Merchant can even broker deals to trade for skill talent swaps (e.g. we will help you prune your fruit trees if we can see your dentist, etc.). The Merchant can also have responsibilities of support or leadership in any of the other Tribe core skill sets. Some of his/her duties can be as simple and routine as making sure that the Provisioner has enough fuel and water for daily cooking, etc.

You knew that <u>the Protector</u> had to be in this group of necessary core skill-sets. Let's lead with a scripture from Jesus in Luke 3:14. "Likewise the soldiers asked him, saying, 'And what shall we do?' So he (Jesus) said to them, 'Do not intimidate anyone or accuse falsely, and be content with your wages.'" Jesus <u>did not say</u> you can no longer be a soldier if you want to be my disciple; what He did say was to not abuse their power and instead live righteously. This type of warrior is a sheepdog versus a wolf (both have teeth and claws, but their motivation is the defining difference). The Protectors honorably serve when others with their power would selfishly take. They know how to fight - improvising and persevering to win, they also know how to use weapons, tactics and military-type situation strategy. You can find many of these skills in the United States Army *Ranger Handbook* (Training Circular No. 3-21.76; PIN: 201554-000; ISBN: 9798457607613) available through Amazon. Protectors can also cultivate courage (it is contagious), do concealment, and may excel in leadership and communications, among other skills.

Military experience - including combat - may seem like essentials for this core skill set, but only 1% of Americans are post 9/11 (2001) combat veterans. Instead, you and all of the Tribe members that you can train may need to be warriors at some point, when a season of lawlessness occurs near you. Protectors can be both men and women who uphold the <u>Warrior Code</u> of protecting the righteous Tribe that they serve in spite of the danger to themselves. An initial testing by fire will forever change their capabilities. They are like sheepdogs who guard the flock with their teeth and claws against the evil wolfs' teeth and claws. They may be armed identically, but their motivation of righteous serving vs. selfish taking is the difference.

You may think that your chances of survival are diminished without everyone being a soldier. My wife and daughters might not be considered soldiers in most armies, but they are warriors when they need to be (just think of the danger of coming between a mother bear and her cubs)! Remember also our pioneer history of women who were not afraid to shoot (and may have been better shots than their husbands)! This plays out in our day with shooting competitions in 4-H club, where girls consistently surpass their male counterparts in marksmanship. In the mid 1800s, it was said that "God made all men, but Colt [firearms maker] made them all equal."

To be complete and fair, we will acknowledge that the average man is larger and stronger than the average female. He also is better able to compartmentalize in his brain (all right brain or all left brain). This was a physiological event, due to testosterone in utero, which destroyed many of the interconnections between brain hemispheres (brain sides). Women could say men are brain damaged, but the result is that men don't struggle as much with battle ethics in split-second decisions. Mrs. Noah adds that men are better able to stay focused on "the goal" while women are easily distracted by keeping many plates spinning. She adds that the strength of this ability for women helps them to generally be superior nurturers in family settings.

In full disclosure I never served in the military or police force. I did earn a black belt in karate that was a 3-year training process of physical and mental preparation. I have never been in combat with someone trying to kill me, but sparring (think kick-boxing) was a routine part of karate training. I have therefore not faced the prospect of death in combat, but have dealt with the prospect of death twice in high mountain climbing mishaps. (So I know something of working my way out of a potential death situation to achieve life).

My combat buddies tell me that what usually happens in first combat is that people freeze and don't remember what to do or conversely that the adrenaline and fear combine to make them hyper (shooting all your magazines with no reserves, etc.) when face-to-face with the possibility of death. Physically realistic training, such as paintball running and hiding with hard breathing, and then shooting may help to get out of the simple target shoot mode. My combat veteran friends tell me that you are always scared, but that courage is "making the butterflies fly in formation".

Another thing they relayed is that your physical senses are heightened so that you see, hear and smell things that sometimes you keep remembering even after you are safe. Personally, I have only read about the incredible carnage of battle and the extraordinary feats of valor in continuing to fight while wounded (e.g. *Against All Odds: A True Story of Ultimate Courage And Survival in World War 2*; Kershaw).

You may go hunting, on reconnaissance missions, and set protective ambushes (or other asymmetric warfare) where camouflage is important to not be seen. *The Art of War* book says that "All warfare is based on deception" - so deception is a useful tactical advantage. Examples would be appearing as a strong force when you are actually weak (the Bible story of Gideon), or not being seen when you are really there, etc. In everyday life I try and live by the scripture that says: "<u>If it is possible, as much as depends on you, live peaceably with all men</u>" (implies that it is not always possible). ¹⁹ "Beloved, do not avenge yourselves, but *rather* give place to wrath; for it is written, 'Vengeance is Mine, I will repay,' says the Lord" (Romans 12:18-19).

Certainly, you will want to be in the best physical fitness possible (see appendix on functional physical fitness) and be proficient in the weapons that you choose. However, being a warrior also entails mental and spiritual characteristics as well. "And Stephen (Acts 6:2 notes his job as table server), full of faith and power, did great wonders and signs among the people. ⁹ Then there arose some ... disputing with Stephen. ¹⁰ And they were not able to resist the wisdom and the Spirit by which he spoke" (Acts 6:8-10). This is one example of the pen or the spoken word being more powerful and appropriate than the sword.

Isaiah 42:13 says: "The Lord shall go forth like a mighty man; He shall stir up His zeal like a man of war. He shall cry out, yes, shout aloud; He shall prevail against His enemies". In the same way when you must fight, have the mindset of a mighty man, and stir up His spirit within you, as you let loose your battle cry and win against the enemies of your Tribe. Proverbs 21:31 reminds us: "The horse is prepared for the day of battle (your part), But deliverance *is* of the LORD."

Also remember that in every battle there are always at least two fights. The first fight is to win the victory and the second fight is to keep the victory (this principle is also true in spiritual battles). The warrior is an over-comer of challenges, of the past (resolve these now if you have not already done so), the present, and in the future to come. "For whatever is born of God overcomes the world. And this is the victory that has overcome the world - our faith." (1 John 5:4).

David illustrates the relationship between the Protector and reliance on the Lord in Psalm 18:1-3: "I will love You, O LORD, my strength.[2] The LORD is my rock and my fortress and my deliverer; My God, my strength, in whom I will trust; My shield and the horn of my salvation, my stronghold.[3] I will call upon the LORD, who is worthy to be praised; So shall I be saved from my enemies." Psalm 18:17-19 continues with: "He delivered me from my strong enemy, From those who hated me, For they were too strong for me.[18] They confronted me in the day of my calamity, But the LORD was my support.[19] He also brought me out into a broad place; He delivered me because He delighted in me."

In verse 34 David says: "<u>He teaches my hands to make war</u>, So that my arms can bend a bow of bronze" (infers great strength); verse 39 continues: "For You have armed me with strength for the battle; You have subdued under me those who rose up against me." Verse 48 concludes: "He delivers me from my enemies. You also lift me up above those who rise against me; You have delivered me from the violent man." There is more to be read in the other parts of that Psalm and other Psalms as well. However, what is clearly shown here is that God uses people (you and your Tribe) to fight physical battles while being with you, for you, and around you - as <u>you</u> are required to <u>fight</u>. If your Christian image struggles with this concept then read David's Psalm 18: 37-39. "I have pursued my enemies and overtaken them; Neither did I turn back again till they were destroyed.[38] I have wounded them, So that they could not rise. They have fallen under my feet.[39] For

You have armed me with strength for the battle; You have subdued under me those who rose up against me."

When you must attack: always strike with surprise, hit as quickly and hard as you can and keep repeating as many times as is necessary to subdue the enemy of your Tribe. You are attempting to catch these "wolves" unprepared and unable to marshal forces quickly enough to respond - hit so hard and repetitively that they panic and are overrun.

<u>The Provisioner</u> is a title that I invented to highlight the duties of the person(s) that maintain the home-base fires and especially keep the Tribe fed (now and future food preservation). Most members of the Tribe will do parts of the Provisioner job at least some times, because of the sheer volume of work that is required to keep a Tribe adequately clothed, fed, etc. Even an army needs to eat and sleep (cook, quartermaster), occasionally clean up (wash, sew, etc.), as well as teach and care for the young ones that are part of our Tribe. It is never too soon to start training your children and grandchildren on various skills and a good work ethic. At the same time, the Provisioner is teaching and modeling how to get along with people and have a good attitude (gratitude-attitude).

In the same way, the Provisioner may also have major responsibilities in other areas (Master-gardener, Medical, Mechanic, Merchant, Protector, Priest, and possibly other Pre-crisis job skills). He or she may have young adults apprentice with others in the Tribe with skills that he/she personally lacks.

As an Eagle Scout on our mountain camping trips I might plan the menus, cook the food - or better yet oversee younger scouts as they learned to cook over an open campfire. I would be charged with seeing that all were warm and dry with their equipment intact and then teach the planned skills for that day. My wife did more of the Provisioner role as our kids were growing up, so I'll have her address the routine skills of this job.

In feeding the Tribe, it will be much harder to cook a meal without always running to the grocery store. Much of the food to be cooked from storage may be different, such as dehydrated foods or textured vegetable protein (tvp). It will take experience to put an acceptable meal on the table and pleasing peoples' palates may not always be possible. Cooking dried beans and rice takes a long time, but even longer if all that is available is an open fire or "rocket stove".

A cast iron pot with a lid (Dutch oven) can theoretically replace the modern stove. Find a large, preferably footed, cast iron Dutch oven and cast iron frying pan (they should be heavy and may possibly be antiques). These must be cleaned and reconditioned or they will be a nightmare to cook with. Bread may have to be ground from wheat, leavened with yeast, and baked in the Dutch oven. Even proficient cooks are going to find this initially difficult. It would be wise to obtain written materials now (may not always have internet later) on frontier cooking over open fires and preparing game. Perhaps practicing some of these recipes now will save panic later.

Large amounts of heated water (for washing dishes, clothes and people) will require large pots. Clothing will wear out, be outgrown and need repair. Begin to accumulate sewing supplies: needles, thread, buttons and fabric. Shop Goodwill stores for heavy jeans for your family – outdoor work is hard on clothing. Mr. Noah wears out jeans every two months in farm season.

Stock up on simple bar soap like old-fashioned IVORY. It has fewer additives and can be used for all ages and all purposes (hair washing, etc.). Wash cloths make taking sponge baths easier. Coconut oil is not only good for cooking, but also for skincare. One of the most used tools on the homestead is a 5-gallon bucket. Keep several for food projects, washing clothes, carrying water, harvesting produce and feeding animals. A good wheelbarrow will save your back. Think of all the things you might do to care for your family and Tribe. Figure out what tools you will need and start looking for these items at garage and estate sales, flea markets and thrift stores, and on-line for used as well as new internet shopping.

If we don't have internet or TV then a well stocked library will be needed. Start with a Bible for each Tribe member. Reference books:

gardening, animal husbandry, homesteading, frontier cooking, sewing, mechanics, building stuff (sheds, fences, etc.), medical care and sanitation, etc. Other reads - favorite fiction, inspiration, history and children's books. Children need to learn reading, writing and arithmetic and can be homeschooled as necessary. (All of our kids were homeschooled for parts of their foundational academic career and later achieved professional degrees in college). Classic games (checkers, chess, cards, etc.), jigsaw puzzles, and balls for various games are all therapeutic for kids' and adults' emotional health.

The Priest: My final regular core skill set, which I consider to be vital to every Tribe, (and hopefully the majority of individuals), is that of a Priest. This may be a totally foreign concept to most, so let me explain what a Priest should contribute. Daniel 11:32 says: "...but the people who know their God shall be strong, and carry out great exploits." He or she is spiritually gifted according to the Bible (see 1 Corinthians chapters 12 and 14) and lives out a daily honorable lifestyle (including prayer, Bible study, praise and worship). Note that most Priests will probably not have theology degrees, but they probably will have many years of Biblical training in Sunday Schools and church, as well as personal Bible study and prayer at the "feet of Jesus". They must have a strong personal relationship with the Lord that actually provides a spiritual covering for those under their care. Read the amazing spiritual history and protection of the early American colonists in the book called *The Light and the Glory* by Marshal and Manuel (ISBN: 0-8007-5054-3).

If you are called to serve your Tribe in this spiritual capacity you must have a very close and committed personal relationship with the Lord and then develop a good set of Priestly skills. See Appendix K: Priest – List of Biblical Foundations. Four groups that will definitely need your Priestly skill-sets are children (*Egermeier's Bible Story Book* – ISBN 978-1-59317-336-4); marriages (Eggerichs' *Love and Respect: the Love She Most Desires, the Respect He Desperately Needs* – ISBN 978-1-59145-187-7); new converts (we have a case of pocket *New Testament Psalms/Proverbs*; and your Tribe prayer warriors (Jackson's *Needless Casualties of War* – ISBN 1-58483-000-X). If you are not a song leader for praise and worship music, then get a pre-recorded song list, hymnal or praise song book. You are to model the life of Jesus as a "servant-leader". Jesus washed the dirty feet of His disciples, and in the same line of reasoning – no needed task is beneath you!

Practice the spiritual principle of sowing and reaping as found in Galations 6: 7-9. "Do not be deceived, God is not mocked; for whatever a man sows, that he will also reap. [8] For he who sows to his flesh will of the flesh reap corruption, but he who sows to the Spirit will of the Spirit reap everlasting life. [9] And let us not grow weary while doing good, for in due season we shall reap if we do not lose heart." If you are strictly thinking in terms of money and physical goods then memorize Luke 6:38 "Give, and it will be given to you: good measure, pressed down, shaken together, and running over will be put into your bosom. For with the same measure that you use, it will be measured back to you." In actuality, there are many hundreds more scriptures and you will spend your lifetime finding and applying them.

Priests are spiritual warriors who fight in the unseen realm, but they may also fight in the natural (consider the example of King David – a musician who served God and yet had much blood on his warrior hands). They should truly understand God's ways and hear from Him on important matters. Your goal is to receive these words when you enter His glory: "His lord said to him, 'Well done, good and faithful servant; you have been faithful over a few things, I will make you ruler over many things. Enter into the joy of your lord.'" Matthew 25:23

Priests may also serve as mediators, judges, leaders, counselors, teachers and encouragers to name a few more duties. If this is unlike any Priest you have ever known then begin to search for one like this now or even become that Priest yourself.

<u>Pre-crisis job skills (and other income sources)</u>: Maybe you see a core skill set that will be essential in this season of self-sufficiency or small group sufficiency that I missed? <u>Pre-crisis job skills</u>, is a broad catch-all for any other job skill or income source not previously discussed related to this season of crisis. Only you know what additional job skills you have that can be used to keep your pre-crisis job or create a

new source of income. Some jobs may remain unaffected in demand while others may cease to exist (at least for this season). Was your job declared "essential" during COVID, or were you forced to quarantine? Perhaps, you have a needed job skill that was formerly just a hobby such as a gunsmith or a guard dog trainer, etc. that can be more fully pursued in the crisis season. Pre-crisis job skills may even be Community in nature versus just the Tribe unit.

In the past, I was an annual guest lecturer at a class for high school graduating seniors. They asked me: "How do I choose a career path?" I answered, "What do you like to do, and where does your passion lie; are you really good at this; does it meet a true need; and will someone actually pay you for doing this?" If the answer is NO to any of these questions then what you have is a good avocation versus a career choice (paying/livable job). Ask yourself – will people be hurt without this service I provide, or conversely will their quality of life be substantially improved? Will someone else feed me so that I can provide my service to others? Without the thin veneer of civilization, will my services even be able to operate in this season?

Will social services and charities still be functional in a collapsed economy (you can speculate, but I wonder if they will eventually return to private vs. governmental sources)? Otherwise, skills that people will pay you for or the ability to do labor (certainly physical and hopefully mental labor) are your meal ticket in this season, but some jobs may be sporadic in having work. The Apostle Paul's admonition is "...if anyone will not work, neither shall he eat" (2 Thessalonians 3:10).

What if I have a pension, retirement funds, social security, alimony, rental income or other cash flow – fantastic if you can count on it continuing? Do consider having at least some of your savings in tangible (physical) assets versus paper assets. <u>Not being in debt</u> is generally a good idea in most economies and reflects on the words of Proverbs 22:7. "The rich rules over the poor, And the borrower is servant to the lender." If you still have your regular job, or you have developed another job with your skills, then you will be less dependent on stored resources.

As you look over this core skill set list of Master-gardener, Medical, Mechanic, Merchant, Protector, Provisioner, Priest, and Pre-crisis job skills, how many of these core skill-sets do you personally cover? Alternatively, could you serve as a secondary back-up in several of these core skills (or learn more about them from the Appendices)? Who in your proposed or current Tribe has what you are lacking or do you need to search out another potential Tribe member? Could other small Tribes in your immediate geographical area serve as a local Community for some of these skill sets? Could things really get so bad that the present system of services will not function the same as they do now, or even stop functioning for a season of time?

Also know that you may consider these core skill sets as "jobs that I do" versus "who I really am" in today's thinking. Do not look down on yourself if you serve others and yourself in these areas that you perhaps never planned on. For most of us, this will be a vital, but relatively short season of your entire life. Prepare Now!

Chapter 4: Transportation, Fuel and Shelter Structures

Transportation needs and fuel requirements (especially to cook and stay warm) as well as shelter structures need their own chapter because they are necessary for quality of life, but don't really fit within the GEAR category. The most basic item for transportation is going to be a pair of sturdy walking shoes or boots, and everyone needs to invest in these. There are also a variety of front and rear packs for carrying small children as well as jogging strollers and wagons (kids are heavy to carry in your arms).

A bicycle is the most efficient mechanism to turn muscle energy into locomotion. Most bikes travel best on a road and can pull a bike trailer (kids or gear), or there are three wheeled trikes/bicycles that combine the elements of bike and trailer together. You can also purchase a rear bike rack for carry tasks. Mountain bikes can be used for off-trail and trail riding. Some newer bikes even have an electric power assist. You can also get a bike light that is powered by a small generator as you pedal for riding at night. Don't forget bike tube patches, spare tubes and a tube pump that attaches to the bike. You will definitely need a heavy chain and bike lock in the coming season.

If you live in an environment with sufficient snow then ice skates (rivers/lakes), cross-country skis, or snowshoes were probably used for transportation in previous generations. Wagons, litters, sleighs, or sleds pulled by horses or dogs might be the next step up. Warm water environments may use flippers (for swimmers) or water craft - row boats, canoes, rafts, sails or motor-craft (if you have fuel). Scooters, all-terrain vehicles (ATVs), powered dirt bikes and motor cycles come in a wide variety of sizes and power capabilities and can be fuel efficient compared to a car or truck.

If you have rural forage/feed, don't overlook riding on animals – donkeys, mules and horses that were the transportation mainstay of yesteryear. Cars, trucks and tractors have great pulling power or carrying capacity and their fuel requirements can vary from gas, diesel, natural gas or electric hybrids. These fuels may be more or less available in your geographic area, so you will need to consider what a viable choice might be.

I have always had fuel available at a more or less affordable price except in the 1973-74 oil embargo. During this time period, gas stations simply did not have gas or rationed you to eight gallons and the waiting lines were very long. It was extremely inconvenient and you never knew if you were even going to get any gas or not that day.

Storing gasoline and diesel safely is not easy. The first thing to do is always keep your vehicle tanks full. Store additional fuels in plastic containers specifically designed for them or in an approved metal storage tank (these typically come in 100 - 1,000 gallon tanks). Tank fuel storage is typically limited to farms and businesses. If you are in town, check with local fire departments on safety storing suggestions.

A couple of ideas that our fire department liked were storing gas cans in a metal filing cabinet or a mesh metal cabinet away from the house with a shed roof covering. Another great idea is to bury a short cement pipe vertically (such as used for a septic system) in the yard and place the cans in its empty center with a lid (you may have to make this yourself out of fire resistant board). Finally, take note that gas or diesel that is stored for longer periods (as little as six months to a year, will need to be stabilized to keep from separating and gumming up your engine). Products to be used preventatively here include Sta-bil fuel stabilizer.

A few may desire to <u>research making their own fuel</u>. I have not personally done this (yet), but you can learn how to make fuel from You-Tube videos. One source is "How to Make Everything" with host Andy George. He tells us it is possible to make your own gasoline (from coal or oil), biodiesel (from animal fats, vegetable fats, or other plant materials), and to make alcohol – ethanol or methanol (from corn or other grains, fruit, and fruit juice).

Sources of energy to make electricity for the home include solar, wind, geothermal, natural gas, and hydropower (the electrical power is stored in batteries for later use). Solar panels on a house (with batteries for storage and an inverter to change DC to AC current) are an idea to seriously consider. Check with your power company to see if tax subsidies are available to pay for some of the initial cost.

Unless you have lots of solar panels, realize that you may only able to alternate power between essential items in your house such as the microwave, electric kettle, stove, kitchen outlets, refrigerator, freezer, computer, and washing machine. Still, this could put you at second-world living status versus the drudgery of third-world. Fuel oil, kerosene, diesel, coal, natural gas, and propane are typical fuels used to heat in the winter. Your home furnace may use one of these fuels, or you may purchase a portable unit (check for ventilation requirements as carbon monoxide can be life threatening).

However, burning wood is by far the most common way to heat your home independently and to cook. A wood burning stove, or a stove insert in an existing fireplace, makes this fuel efficient (add catalytic converters for pollution control). Note that for safety, the stove and piping should be inspected and cleaned of creosote at least annually.

We have a copper kettle on our stove to put moisture back into the dry room air. We also have a mechanical fan (no electricity) that sits on the stove and spins itself due to the heat on the metal fins.

Harvesting wood yourself requires some tools, but is much more affordable than buying split wood retail. Tools could include an axe, maul, splitting wedges, hatchet, and bow saw on the manual side. Power tools could include a chainsaw (probably gas powered, but there are electric and battery powered models). A powered wood splitter (probably gas powered) saves significant time and muscle energy, but consider a unit that runs off the PTO (power take-off of a tractor) if available. These power tools come in various sizes and power ranges. All these tools have safety requirements and protective equipment is needed (leather gloves, goggles, hearing protection, face shield, hard hat and chainsaw protective chaps).

Keeping the wood dry is important for easy burning, so stack and tarp or shelter the wood. Soft woods (pine, cottonwood, etc.) are less dense and burn up quicker and produce less heat than hard woods. Note that you should not underestimate the amount of wood that can be burned in a winter. You should also consider building your own "rocket stove" for outdoor use - simple to do with a few portable stackable bricks. It efficiently burns little scraps of wood for cooking and heat (definitely You-Tube this item and try it out for yourself).

Many people already own a charcoal or propane grill for outdoor cooking (maybe stock up on these fuels). Some sunny climate people really like solar ovens (relatively simple design to make or buy). Alternatives include sterno cans, small gas powered cook stoves, and the early Western pioneers cooked with dried animal dung. Finally, unless you plan on going to bed as soon as it gets dark, you will need lighting. Candles come to mind, but lanterns (lamp oil or battery powered) are much easier to read by. Consider fire safety with flame.

Shelter - in a winter environment, your first layer of shelter is personal clothing. Start with long-johns, wool socks, wool shirt and pants, or flannel lined shirt and pants. Outerwear includes a goose down vest, wool scarf or balaclava (head/neck covering only showing the face), and neoprene face mask (covers nose and cheeks), goggles, wool hat, wool sweater, gloves that can go inside of mittens, and a heavy jacket (water and wind proof), with a hood if you prefer.

The head and neck area is where most body heat is lost and the body will pull blood from the extremities to pool blood in the trunk for your survival. However, we know that we are not going to freeze, so we want this blood to go back to our fingers and toes. We can therefore get blood and warmth back into our fingers and toes by putting on a wool hat, scarf, etc. to prevent heat loss from the head. Dress in layers and minimize sweating – clothing made with "Thinsulate" or "Gore-Tex" both insulate and are breathable to let moisture out. If your hands and feet get cold easily, you may want to consider chemical reaction warmer packets (one-time disposable or reusable packets when placed back in boiling water).

More people run into major life threats from hypothermia - lowering of core body temperature; (treatment covered in Medical appendix) when outside than for any other reason. Therefore, we will teach you how to build a quick survival shelter in the wilderness with a minimum of equipment.

Bush-crafting is taking tree limbs and evergreen boughs to make a lean-to structure. One example is to place a large branch (body length or longer) at an inclined angle (laying it against a big rock, the fork in a tree, etc.) for the lean-to opening. The ribs of this structure are made by laying limbs on either side of the main spine for its entire length (triangle shaped length). The ribs are then covered with evergreen boughs, matted leaf clumps or patches of moss, etc. to make a wind and moisture barrier. To keep off of the cold ground, you can lay down pine boughs or lay down additional tree limbs. This project can be accomplished with just a saw (regular, bow, or metal rope saw), hatchet or machete (a little rope may also be helpful).

In the winter, with heavy snow around, an igloo type structure can be built with just a shovel. One simple design is to make a pile of snow (your body length) and tramp it down under foot. Next, dig out a doorway at ground level, just big enough for you to squeeze through. Dig this tunnel to the back of the dome and create some ceiling space. If you will be sleeping in this structure, then dig out the space above your raised beds on either side of the tunnel. (Coldest air will stay in the tunnel and the warmer air will rise to the ceiling). Also dig a small air vent in the roof to let out your carbon dioxide.

<u>Portable Shelters</u> allow protection from the elements that can be carried with you if you need to leave your home. Arctic tents (a pyramid style tent like in the TV show M.A.S.H.) or a tipi is available by special order and can have a stove inside. You can pitch a pup tent (Ridge/A-frame like in civil war movies) inside of a cabin tent (tall enough to stand in) for trapping heated air (Eagle Scout trick). I have camped every month of the year in the Rocky Mountains, even in snow, and it is cold living (but you can earn your Polar Bear award!).

Family cabin tents can come with multiple rooms for families. There are also tree hammock tents and bivy tents (one person ground tent), dome tents, tunnel tents, and geodesic tents (all describe shape) that stand up well to big wind. Constructing a physical wind break to shield one or two sides of your tent is what ranchers do for their livestock. However, don't plan on living in a tent long-term unless you live in a more moderate climate. If you live in a house, cabin, Mongolian yurt (think round canvas covered stick house), apartment, trailer or other permanent structure consider adding insulation to increase energy efficiency. You can plant a windbreak to cut winter's wind and shade trees to decrease the sun's heat in summer for a permanent structure.

<u>Factors for you to consider in deciding to move for family safety.</u> Realistically consider, if you live in a <u>neighborhood</u> that will be safe in a crisis situation, and then provide further <u>security enhancements</u> (stronger locks and metal or security doors, metal hinge protectors, window security, non-electric security systems, etc.). Can you get to know your neighbors now and establish a "neighborhood watch?" If, in the future, your location is no longer safe, then be prepared to quickly

move out. Plan now for a reachable get-away location and stock it now with as many supplies as possible. Some may have the option of moving to a more secure area with family or extremely good friends, but discuss this in advance of the crisis. Do not wait until travel is no longer safe, or fuel is unavailable. The very short window for safe travel is considered to be when significant disruption is still considered "only temporary" by most people.

Seriously consider if you should move your stuff and life even now to establish a safer location and avoid a panic scramble later. As a general rule of thumb, smaller towns should be safer than larger cities in a crisis. Rural land should also be safer than bigger cities, but it may take a number of people (your Tribe) to adequately defend.

<u>Rural land – things you would need to know</u> if you are considering this type of move. If you decide to look for rural land, consider the following questions: Is this land only a get-away location from desperate people – a survival hideout? Alternatively, is the land good for growing food or raising livestock, or perhaps very good hunting and/or fishing? Does it already have some infrastructure like a passable road (or is any road seasonal only)? Does it have a livable house (trailer, modular, cabin, stick construction) or what would it take to make it livable? Does it have a shed(s) or other outbuildings for storage and animals? Does it have a basement or storm shelter that could function as a security bunker?

Fencing is highly variable in form and function, but can it keep animals in and some people out? Does it have a well for water (or how hard will it be to dig or drill one) if surface water such as a spring, stream, or lake is not nearby? If the water table is high enough, you may be able to drill your own well with PVC pipe or a metal sand point. What are the surrounding neighbors like? Are they also independently prepared, good people, and would they be willing to trade help with you if necessary?

Maybe you can convince friends and family to move with you to adjoining land so that you bring additional support with you (think new

Tribe). Just so you know, "it takes money to live poor in the country" as many living costs are more expensive. Will decreased city housing costs and taxes offset some of these increases? How do other people in the area make a living, and can you make a living there? (Consider internet, phone service, mail service, and delivery requirements). Did you know that poor internet service is the number one complaint of rural dwellers? How easily can you adjust to living (for at least a season) without some of the services and amenities that you enjoyed in the city? The best time to plan and execute such a move is yesterday, so if this is your plan, don't wait until it is too late!

Chapter 5: Pure Water, Sanitation and Communication

The purification of water is as important as things can get (3 days without water is probably fatal). Water that is contaminated with chemicals (pesticides, herbicides, fertilizers), bacteria, viruses, protozoa, fecal matter, heavy metals, and other contaminants can cause diarrhea, parasites, poisoning, hepatitis-A, typhoid, and cholera (not to mention bad taste). Sediment in the water can be reduced by gravity (letting water sit and skim water off the top, mechanical filtration (very fine sieve to trap the sediment), or even a coffee filter (cloth handkerchief or T-shirt in the wilderness). However, this is only the first step as it does not actually disinfect the water. Chlorine dioxide tablets can disinfect water in about 30-minutes. Water filters more quickly trap the bacteria, parasites, and chemical contaminates (including industrial solvents), if you need a drink now.

1. Reverse Osmosis (RO) is a membrane that catches these contaminates and takes them away with a back flush.

2. Ceramic filters have very small holes that let water through, but not the larger contaminants. This could be a good choice for a Tribe.

3. Activated carbon and paper filters are a less pricey method, but the cylinders must be periodically replaced. In a camp situation, you can make your own campfire charcoal and wrap it in a cloth. You then cover the cloth with sand and then pebbles in a container with a small

hole at the bottom and a catch bucket beneath it. The filtered water will leak out slowly and should be repeated 2-3 times before drinking.

4. Chemical Disinfection is using chlorine dioxide, or less commonly now iodine, usually in tablet form to kill viruses, bacteria and pathogens. Wait 30-minutes before drinking the water with chemical disinfection methods (know that there may be some aftertaste).

5. Ozone (03) filtration is an oxidant that is more potent than chlorine in inactivating fungus and other organics, viruses, pesticides and contaminates such as sulfur and iron. It is the most used filtration system worldwide for communities.

6. Solar water disinfection uses full sunlight to kill pathogens. This is done by placing your water in clear bottles on a dark surface for about 6 hours (can take two cloudy days).

7. UV (ultra-violet) lamps and pens need clear water to kill bacteria and viruses in just a few minutes. This is a very small and light weight unit that backpackers may carry with them.

8. Distillation requires capturing the steam from boiled water (contaminants are left behind; think of it as a still for water).

9. Boiling water is the old standby gold standard to kill parasites, pathogens, and micro-organisms in just 1-minute (rolling boil).

In earlier chapters we talked about food and cooking, but we have yet to discuss the potentially difficult issues of ongoing sanitation and human waste management. If the power and/or water are out how will you bathe, flush toilets, or otherwise get rid of body waste? Yes, a good store of toilet paper is important, but how did the pioneers survive without TP? A couple of generations ago they used catalogue paper and an outhouse.

In the country, we have built a nice portable outhouse, for emergencies, with a 5-gallon catch bucket. The bucket has a screw on lid and could be dumped in the septic system. In town, could you physically dump your sewage into the underground sewage system? Could you use the same bucket system and pour the waste into the toilet for flushing (even if the water is off)? You should be able to use the toilet and flush it (sparingly) by pouring in water as the plumbing is still connected to the sewer.

In desperate situations (or camping), you can use a hand trowel to dig a cat-hole or a latrine ditch for a group. Rigging up a privacy curtain and having some lime (calcium oxide) and dirt to cover the waste, can work for quite some time. The problem comes if that waste is left exposed to flies as an open sewer or is washed into a water supply. Diseases such as cholera can result and are serious health issues. The military often burns its waste in a barrel or metal trough. (Did you know that twice as many soldiers died of disease rather than combat wounds in the Civil War)? Modern composting toilets may be another option. If you run low on TP, you can gather leaves, etc., but watch out for poison ivy! Pioneers would also use rags that were then placed in a bucket; washed and reused (this same system was also used for feminine hygiene). We foresee many writing up a shopping list to try and avoid these more primitive measures.

Personal hygiene discussions include how do you clean up without a plumbed shower (we assume that you have a supply of soap)? In the warmer months, you can place water in a "solar water bag" that is black and heated by the sun. Pioneer families would occasionally heat and pour water into a bowl for a sponge bath, or a real bath (where the water could be shared by the entire family – one after another). If you have a lake or stream and reasonable temperature, then you are very fortunate.

Cleaning your clothes might be accomplished by boiling them in a pot, using a ripple washboard, or pounding on river rocks? Alternatively, clothes can be placed in a 5-gallon bucket and using a toilet plunger for agitation. For very small loads, we have heard about a sealed globe that is turned by hand to agitate the wash. Drying clothes is the greater problem as they would be dried on a clothes line. An old fashioned hand wringer saves much hard labor getting the water out (these are available new).

How do you wash dishes without a dishwasher? Prepare two tubs of very hot water (rubber gloves are needed). First scrape the foods scrapes into a bucket (or have your dog lick them – ha!) and then wash dishes with liquid soap in the first tub. Rinse the dishes in the second tub (put in a splash of bleach) and dry those on a dish rack or hand dry them with a dish rag.

Ok, so then what do you do without (or sporadic) trash service? Many older neighborhood houses use to have a cement incinerator (or even a 50-gallon drum in the backyard) to burn their household waste. The ashes were later buried or even used in the garden as a nutrient if they were clean. If this seems old fashioned, then you might not believe that later on, inmate trustees went out on trash collection trucks, and some were even chained to the back of the truck! Trash was collected from the side of the roads in the same way. Seriously though, trash must be bagged (put this on your gear list) and disposed of on a regular basis or mice, vermin, flies, and other disease carriers are a very real public health threat.

<u>Communication</u> is the other subject that needs to be covered in this chapter. Cell phones are great as long as satellites and relay towers are functioning. If they are not, or the circuits are simply overloaded, your cell phone won't work. Landlines are few and far between these days, and most of us don't have military-grade satellite phones. Fortunately, there are still people who operate HAM radio stations. They may have massive antennas and repeater connections that enable them to reach throughout the country and into the world.

Simple handheld HAM equipment with a small, attached antenna can be purchased for as little as $100. You will need to study and take a test for a technician license to be legal (and get your own call sign). However, this is a great communication tool when cell phones fail. There are higher levels of licensing (General and Extra license) and HAM equipment that cost hundreds or even thousands of dollars. Maybe your Tribe offers this service for trade or vice versa?

Any licensed HAM (levels are technician, general and the extra classification), have increasing broadcasting privileges. After passing the written test(s), all will need actual field experience. Many cities and geographic areas have HAM radio clubs that can help average people to get started and use these tools. CB (citizen band) radios that are routinely seen in trucker cabs and some enthusiasts' cars and trucks, are another communication device that may work when cells are down. CBs generally don't have licensing requirements, but do have some etiquette rules to follow (you got it – learn this from You-Tube). Various types of walkie-talkies are relatively inexpensive (at the entry point, but can be pricey at higher ends) and may be able to connect two or more people within line-of-sight for a half-mile or even greater distances.

Whether or not any or all of these systems would be disabled with an EMP (electromagnetic pulse) weapon is unknown and controversial. Signal lights for Morse code and signal flags were important (and probably still are as a back-up) to the military. Hand signals are useful for silent communication in tactical situations and can be learned once again on the internet. American Sign Language could be another useful communication skill to learn for some.

Chapter 6: Body, Mind and Spirit Strategies for Surviving Crisis Times

It is my belief that I am a spirit, I have a soul (mind, will and emotions), and I live in a body. All three parts of my being must be cared for to survive and optimally thrive.

Functional Physical Fitness: I believe that most of us would agree that we are not as physically fit as our grandparents were. In the coming chaos season we will probably be required to do some very physical things as part of everyday living. In college, I visited my cousins on the farm and asked them where they worked out. I was a disciplined competitive athlete, but they looked every bit as fit as me - the gym rat. They laughed and said – "bucking hay bales" as they proceeded to take me to their gym!

You could lift bricks on a stick, canned goods in a reusable grocery sack, or use the weights at home or the gym and get the same results. So exercise can be in various forms as long as it produces an "overload" so that the body physically adapts to the significantly increased workload. Note that if the muscles are not required to do more than you can do now then they won't need to change. The second principle is "progression" – meaning that you add overload stress incrementally. If you want to be able to jog a mile, you first walk at whatever level you are able (maybe it's just once around the block that first week and walking that mile after a month?). The third principle is "warm-up and cool-down". You wouldn't start your car on a freezing morning and then burn-rubber to take off. Machines don't work that way and neither does your body. Do gentle whole body movement and then a little stretching (do not bounce or jerk to stretch) as a part of cool-down. The fourth principle is "specificity" – meaning if I want to firm up my abdominal muscles then I target movement there (e.g. modified sit-up) and if I want to work on my biceps (e.g. biceps arm curl).

So what are the body systems that need to be shaped up? Let's start with the cardiovascular system (heart and lungs). These improvements come from walking, jogging, running, swimming, whole body continuous movement games (tennis, soccer, paddleball, racquetball, basketball, etc.). The second body system to train is the musculoskeletal system. Skeletal muscles work to increase their strength (activities like lifting kids or grocery sacks, lifting heavy bricks, etc.). Skeletal muscles increase their muscle endurance by chopping wood or lifting smaller things repeatedly – like stacking wood, etc. The most common way to work on muscle strength and muscle endurance without equipment is callisthenic exercises (sit-ups, push-ups, etc.). If you have some hand held weights at home then find a buddy to lift with.

Muscle strength can also be increased through isometric exercises (requiring no equipment). For example, if you are seated in a chair, pull up on the seat of the chair while sitting in it. The chair will not move, but the biceps muscles will work (hold for 6-seconds and then relax and repeat). Another example is to clasp both hands together and push against each other for 6-seconds (no limb movement occurs while the muscle is working). So understand that you can work out anywhere without equipment.

Skeletal muscles also need to maintain their flexibility (stretch-ability) through gentle muscle stretching. Stretch each muscle individually by extending it to its full range of movement (you should feel muscle tension, but not pain). Hold that full muscle tension for at least 5 seconds without bouncing or jerking. Repeat a second time and proceed on to the next muscle. Body composition is the amount of fat (that I want to lose) or the muscle size I want to gain. Muscle size increase is a result of lifting heavier weights/resistance and having the primarily male hormone testosterone (females have less testosterone).

The US has an obesity crisis with about 42% of all Americans being obese (excessive body fat) and over 9% of these are severely obese according to the CDC (Centers for Disease Control). Obesity is considered to be the "new smoking risk factor" for various degenerative diseases. Obesity is linked with heart disease, stroke, diabetes, various cancers, joint problems, and a host of other medical issues. Therefore, shedding this excess fat is preventative medicine for your future. Obesity is also a main reason that recruits wash out of military boot-camp.

At its most basic level, body fat loss is a result of burning up fat with oxygen (heavy breathing) in cardio activities. Decreased body fat is also a result of eating fewer calories than you burn off. However, calorie types are not all the same in this equation and highly processed foods are very problematic. Furthermore, obesity is a complex problem involving heredity, lifestyle, food type availability, financial considerations, cultural and psychological issues. In the absence of severe food shortages, it may be a lifetime struggle for many. We will share a potential breakthrough that may really help.

Timing your eating to minimize the release of insulin (insulin takes calories out of the bloodstream and stores them in fat cells) is the study called "IF". Intermittent fasting reduces your "eating window" (for me that currently means only eating at noon and the second meal finished by 6:00 PM – a 6 hour eating window and an 18-hour fast). This fast period allows for "auto-phage" where the body clears out cellular debris and helps the immune system fight disease. If you need to lose significant weight, then talk with your doctor after reading the book *Fast, Feast, Repeat* by Gin Stephens (ISBN 978-1-250-75762-3). My wife and I have both lost significant weight without undue hunger (particularly if you also give up - or at least minimize sugar and white flour). We have also seen other medical health benefits (decreased cholesterol, decreased blood sugar, etc.), and find this eating system to be sustainable. Some call intermittent fasting (IF) the health lifestyle with weight loss benefits.

Mental/Emotional Health in crisis situations: The soul is your combined mind, will and emotions. It is the part of us that is aware of our own individuality and also relates to others. Our conscious mind is our thinking and reasoning and our subconscious mind may include our memories, feelings, attitudes and beliefs. In chaos situations, your mental/emotional health (state of mind) can be a tremendous asset or a deadly liability.

Proverbs 18:21 tells us: "Death and life are in the power of the tongue, And those who love it will eat its fruit." Your words have power and your brain knows your voice above all other voices. Speak life (positive words) and do not curse yourself with negative words that can become a self-fulfilling prophecy of destruction. Train yourself to speak life into the lives of your children, spouse and Tribe. In John 10:10 we learn - "The thief (satan) cometh not, but for to steal, and to kill, and to destroy: I (Jesus) am come that they might have life, and that they might have it more abundantly". How we counter this is found in James 4:7-8 "Therefore submit to God. Resist the devil and he will flee from you. [8] Draw near to God and He will draw near to you. Cleanse *your* hands, *you* sinners; and purify your hearts, you double-minded" (faith & unbelief mixture).

The determined will to survive is seen in the story of Vietnam POW pilot Colonel Fred Cherry. Tortured 93 days straight, 702 days in solitary, 5 months without medical care (broken wrist, ankle, shoulder) and was a prisoner for 7.5-years. He told the Daily Collegian that fellow prisoner support and mutual faith were the keys to his survival. Proverbs 11:25 tells you that giving to others is refreshment to our soul. "The generous soul will be made rich, And he who waters will also be watered himself." The psychology literature supports the vital concept of the need to maintain hope to survive difficult situations. It goes yet further, to say that the loss of all hope is when people give up and death is more likely to follow.

Stress Management: What are some practical things that you have already discovered as a way to deal with stress situations? I like sitting in front of a warm fire, a hot drink, a warm shower, exercising, walking in nature, singing a song of praise, reading the Bible or another good book (something that shows me a hero to applaud - encouragement for a brief escape). Take a deep breath in and then exhale fully. Don't neglect to give your situation to God as instructed in 1 Peter 5:7 encourages - "Casting all your cares on Him, for He cares for you."

I play games with my grandkids, watch videos and read books to them (think about how you can help them cope with a stress environment). Perhaps you have a spouse that you can confide in or that BFF (best friend forever) confidant, a pastor or other spiritual advisor. All of these illustrate trust and a sense of belonging that reinforces hope. Most importantly, go to the Lord as in Isaiah 26:3 – "You will keep *him* in perfect peace, *Whose* mind *is* stayed *on You*, Because he trusts in You." When you need joy and hope go to the God who not only has those qualities, but indeed is those qualities! Romans 15:13 – "Now may the God of hope fill you with all joy and peace in believing, that you may abound in hope by the power of the Holy Spirit."

Faith vs. Fear: So how do you mentally and emotionally deal with very negative news or circumstances? Jesus told his disciples about the future days (our coming days) in Matthew 24:6-8. "And you will hear of wars and rumors of wars. See that you are not troubled; for all these things must come to pass, but the end is not yet. For nation will rise against nation, and kingdom against kingdom. And there will be famines, pestilences, and earthquakes in various places. All these are the beginning of sorrows." George Washington's vision (for our coming season) of the third great peril is in this future negative news category. I am therefore not shocked when I read in Psalm 34:19 that "Many *are* the afflictions of the righteous, But the LORD delivers him out of them all". John 16:33 then tells us it is possible to have inner peace despite these circumstances - "These things I have spoken to you, that in Me you may have peace. In the world you will have tribulation; but be of good cheer, I have overcome the world."

The US Military "Survival Evasion, Resistance and Escape" manual also urges you to learn what to expect. The strategy is that if you know something is coming, it won't surprise you as much, and you can better prepare emotionally to deal with it. A magazine article on the internet is called "One Year in Hell" and is a graphic firsthand account of a city in the Bosnian War (early 1990's). For a full year they were cut off and surrounded by an army. They had no electric, water, gas, no distribution (food, clothing, etc.), no medical, no police and gangs ruled. If you are trying to imagine what the coming chaos might look like on a day-to-day basis – read this intense, short and informative article. If you need external motivation to prepare – look no further!

Or for a less intense overview you could read the novel *One Second After* by Forstchen. During his time in the US Navy he was given the assignment of postulating what would happen in the US if an EMP (electromagnetic pulse) weapon knocked out all electronics (we would be in 1800's technology). His final prognosis was that only 10% of all Americans would still be alive after one year! <u>Do NOT read either of these to be scared and worry</u>, read them instead to understand what you must do now to prepare to be a survivor later.

<u>Future Hope:</u> Three books that talk about the coming chaos to the US, but show that its final end result is a fabulous new beginning are: *America in the Bible* by Stephen Grant (ISBN: 978-1-4497-5684-0); *In Defense of a Nation* by Stanley Grant (ISBN: 978-1-4497-2917-2); and *Why America Still Matters To God* by Geoffry Broughton (ISBN-13: 978-1976347696). One final book is a blueprint for actually rebuilding the nation based on the principles found in the Bible book of Nehemiah (*Rules for Rebuilders* by Steven Grant and Stanely Grant - ISBN: 978-1-4808-6717-8). These four books emphasize that <u>the chaos period is a</u>

<u>time limited season.</u> The psychological literature reports that if you know that a very difficult situation has an endpoint then it is more bearable. These books can instill hope that our country will ultimately survive and that you can be part of its great rebuilding.

Hans Selye was nominated for a Nobel Prize for his work that demonstrated the mind-body link. To illustrate, if you stumble across the path of a tiger, your body releases stress chemicals that prepare for a fight or flight (run away). In either case the stress chemicals are burned up in the physical action you take. However, if the boss or teacher yells at you and you can't fight or run away, then these stress chemicals circulate in your body and damage it. So when you don't cope with mental stress (endless worrying) then it creates physical issues in your body (dis-ease).

There is also a pastor, Henry W. Wright, who wrote a book called *A More Excellent Way to Be in Health* that explores the link between spiritual issues and their impact on both emotional and then physical health outcomes. For example a "spirit of fear" is dealt with in the scripture that says: "For God has not given us a spirit of fear, but of power and of love and of a <u>sound mind."</u> Faith is the opposite of fear – they both expect a future event (one positive and the other negative)! Fear is an initial reaction, but faith is our chosen response, and our responsibility! Therefore praise could even be seen as the very barometer of your faith, when satan's lie is that God has abandoned you!

Isaiah 26:9 tells us: "With my soul I have desired You in the night, Yes, by my spirit within me I will seek You early..." Therefore, both our soul (mind, will and emotions) as well as our spirit (the part of our tri-unity being that relates directly to God) are cable of seeking the Lord. However, you will need a better theologian than me to explain where soul ends and spirit begins.

<u>Spiritual Health for Crisis Times:</u>

<u>Understanding the spirit of man:</u> Would you agree that most people groups around the world experience conscience (innate sense of right and wrong)? Perhaps you have experienced great intuition (almost an

instinctive feeling - that proved to be right), rather than you're your conscious reasoning? Both of these may be part of your spirit man, but we are certain that our communication with God is birthed (John 3:3) when we invite Jesus into our lives. Romans 8:26 - "Likewise the Spirit also helps in our weaknesses. For we do not know what we should pray for as we ought, but the Spirit Himself makes intercession for us with groanings which cannot be uttered." Romans 8:15-17 – "For you did not receive the spirit of bondage again to fear, but you received the Spirit of adoption by whom we cry out, 'Abba, Father.' [16] The Spirit Himself bears witness with our spirit that we are children of God, [17] and if children, then heirs—heirs of God and joint heirs with Christ, if indeed we suffer with Him, that we may also be glorified together." Our trust and hope has purpose – an essential coping strategy for inner peace of mind and survival.

Victor Frankel was a psychiatrist who survived the holocaust concentration camp and claimed that search for life's meaning is the central human motivational force. If this is true, I choose the Westminster Confession of 1646 - "Man's primary purpose is to glorify God and to delight in Him forever". Why this is important, is that God may take you through some things by His power (and for His glory) that He could have easily saved you from by His providence. This is illustrated in the story of the three Hebrew men (executive staff to the great pagan king of the earth) who were thrown into the fiery furnace because they would not bow down to the king's idol.

Daniel 3:17-18 records their response to the king when they would not bow [17] '...our God whom we serve is able to deliver us from the burning fiery furnace, and He will deliver *us* from your hand, O king. [18] But if not, let it be known to you, O king, that we do not serve your gods, nor will we worship the gold image which you have set up.' So the angry king had them bound and cast into the fiery furnace, but in verse 25 he said: '...I see four men loose, walking in the midst of the fire; and they are not hurt, and the form of the fourth is like the Son of God.' The story is completed in verses 27-29 "...governors and the king's counselors gathered together, and they saw these men on whose bodies the fire had no power; the hair of their head was not singed nor were their garments affected, and the smell of fire was not on them.

[28]Nebuchadnezzar spoke, saying, 'Blessed be the God of Shadrach, Meshach, and Abed-Nego, who sent His Angel and delivered His servants who trusted in Him, and they have frustrated the king's word, and yielded their bodies, that they should not serve nor worship any god except their own God! [29] Therefore I make a decree that ... there is no other God who can deliver like this.'" These men risked their lives, the Lord was glorified, and their story is recounted throughout the ages. Would you risk your life in service to the one Great King or even receive God's "Martyrs Crown"? In my opinion, this one event would make life worth living during the chaos season!

In our own country we have this recorded event. Did you know that Washington should not have even survived the earlier (1755) French and Indian Wars? An Indian Chief came to visit then President Washington and said - "I told my braves to target you and they shot you, but you were not hurt". (Washington reported that he had four musket ball holes through his uniform and yet was untouched). God had a purpose for Washington to fulfill and so it can be with you. Know that the Lord can protect you, even in impossible situations, until His purpose for you is completed. This story and many other miracles of early America are found in the book "The Light and the Glory" by Marshal and Manuel – ISBN: 0-8007-5054-3).

David once found himself in a crisis situation where his own Tribe wanted to stone him because the enemy had captured their families. 1 Samuel 30:6 relates: "Now David was greatly distressed, for the people spoke of stoning him, because the soul of all the people was grieved, every man for his sons and his daughters. But David strengthened himself in the LORD his God." In Psalm 13 (read this in your Bible) we have David's prayer that ultimately turned depression into delight. He was brutally honest with God in his hurting (don't worry – God has big shoulders). David prayed, certainly remembering Gods faithfulness in the past, and praised his way out of despair and on to victory over his mortal enemies. Remember this spiritual lesson in your future as well. Ephesians 3:16 says – "that He would grant you, according to the riches of His glory, to be strengthened with might through His Spirit in the (your) inner man."

Prospect of death without fear: What if I do die in this chaos period - is all hope lost and does God even care? Psalm 116:15 declares: "Precious in the sight of the LORD *Is* the death of His saints." Also 1 Thessalonians 4:15 informs us: "But we do not want you to be uninformed, brethren, about those who are asleep (deceased Christians), so that you will not grieve as do the rest who have no hope." As a Christian you can be confident that to be absent from the body is to be present with the Lord. 2 Corinthians 5:8 - "We are confident, yes, well pleased rather to be absent from the body and to be present with the Lord." Personally, I declare the hope of life as expressed in Jeremiah 29:11, "For I know the thoughts that I think toward you, says the LORD, thoughts of peace and not of evil, to give you a future and a hope."

Chapter 7: Conclusion and Call to Action

Just like Noah and Joseph did in the Bible, we must prepare in this season for the next coming season of intense chaos. Consider the signs of the times: COVID, spiraling food costs (famine in many places), supply chain delays and shortages, severe weather events (floods, hurricanes), massive wildfires, and earth quakes in the current news. Future news will include George Washington's third great peril vision; that is yet to happen (he was right twice before). John Paul Jackson's prophetic warning of "The Coming Perfect Storm" may rip the thin veneer of civilization off of our country. These elements are like sticks of dynamite against the wall of Fortress America. There has been a recent "sea change" where these fuses have now been lit.

1) Political – policy breakdown and corruption;
2) Religious Conflicts – radical intolerance and persecution;
3) Wars – civil and worldwide;
4) Economic – disruption and then collapse;
5) Natural Disasters – both increased magnitude and numbers of geo-physical events. The number of these geophysical events is already 10X greater than in 1960.

Remember that the combined sum of these five elements is magnified/multiplied over what each element could do individually and that they will come in repeated waves. Governments will not be able to adequately respond, so your trust must rest elsewhere.

However, you can take personal responsibility and Prepare Now! You can develop your own 5 Gs plan (Gear; Grub; Greenbacks; Guard-dog; and God-relationship). You can hone your own physical fitness in preparation for physical work, have your bases covered for transportation, fuel, emergency shelter, pure water, sanitation, and communication. You can combine your Tribe (small group of family and/or close friends) skill sets with your own to be "synergistically stronger" than the individual parts. You can all become who you are needed to be in this chaos season (Master-Gardener, Medical, Mechanic, Merchant, Protector, Provisioner, Priest, and any other Pre-crisis job skills) to serve your Tribe and others. The choice is laid out in two simple pages – Appendix L: One Page Preparation Summary or will you chose Appendix M: 12 Reason Not to Prep? Review both of these documents now and make your decision.

Even in the approaching season of chaos, you can be anticipating the very good season following of regenerating your nation). Remember that preparation is the action of faith. Closing word - Finish your "ark" now – the flood is coming soon!

Appendices Index - <u>Finish Your Ark Now</u>: the Prudent Prepper's Primer!

Finish Your Ark Now: the Prudent Prepper's Primer! <u>Appendices A - M</u>

<u>Appendix A: GEAR "bug-out" or "bug-in" pack or bag</u> (packed items):

1. Goose down sleeping bag or poly-fill bags for couples that can zip together (alternatively just pack heavy blankets, preferably wool)

2. Foam pad (old bones don't sleep well on cold dirt, alternatively an air mattress)

3. Flashlight & Batteries   4. Knife & Sharpening stone

5. Hatchet (chop wood, pound stakes)   6. Matches and candle

7. Lighter and/or Metal Match (scrape off metal shavings with a knife and then metal spark to light even in wind/drizzle)

8. Food (Lara/Cliff bars, dried fruit, beef jerky – shelf stable, high calorie, nutrient dense);

9. Water and "Life Straw" personal water filter or chlorine dioxide water treatment tablets   10. Toilet paper

11. Folding shovel or hand trowel (what bears do in the woods?)

12. Small backpacking tent (plastic sheeting if you prefer)

13. Extra clothing: wool socks, jacket & wool hat

14. Sun glasses and sun hat (cover neck and ears)

15. Leather gloves (double as hot pads)   16. Poncho or rain gear

17. Military style can opener, metal cooking cup & spoon or mess kit & stacking flat wear   18. Wire saw or small folding saw

19. Nylon rope and carabineers   20. First-aid kit   21. Compass

22. Bug spray and sunscreen   23. Compact Bible <u>and</u> this book

24. Survival kit (small - with fishing line & hooks, band-aids, whistle, bouillon cubes & tea, water treatment tablets, metal wire, aluminum foil, space blanket). If you always carry a wallet then: (driver's license, insurance cards and Cash - small bills).

Appendix B: Prepare Now - Quick Start

The Prepare Now – Quick Start lets you select one thing to do in each of the categories to get you started immediately. If you want to alter any of the first thing suggestions with your own alternative then great!

Tribe: Have at least one person that lives close and has agreed to partner with you in an emergency. Select a specific place that you could meet if you had to leave your home. Work together to prep plan.

5 Gs of Preparedness:

Gear: Fill a "bug-out" pack or easy carry bag with as many of the gear items (see list) as you presently have on hand.

Grub: Water stored and food on hand for at least two weeks.

Greenbacks: Have at least $200 in small bills ($5, $10, $20) at home.

Guard-dog: Have a means of self protection – dog, pepper spray, or gun

God-relationship: Get to know God on a personal level by daily Bible reading and prayer (talking with God). This should lead you to consider the claims of Jesus - accept Him as your Savior & Lord (boss)

Other general items listed in the book: *get a good pair of walking shoes and start walking   *have a winter jacket, rain coat, wool hat and mittens   *keep your gas tank filled   *get a solar cell phone charger   *have at least one alternate heating method for your home *If you had to leave your home, arrange with friends or family to be each other's backup retreat   *if you plan to shelter outside then have a good tent   *have materials for a camping fire (consider bricks for a "rocket stove"; have a bucket with lid that has a hand trowel and TP; start planning how you would cope emotionally and spiritually in a major life disruption situation.

Core Preparedness Skills:

Master-gardener: Start reading about gardening or find someone with a garden who needs help and start talking.

Medical: Have a home first aid kit and simple first aid reference book

Merchant: Keep some barter items on hand such as coffee, chocolate, cocoa, water purification tablets (chlorine dioxide), lighters, TP, .22, shotgun and other caliber shells, etc.

Mechanic: Purchase a small basic tool kit – duct tape, hammer, pliers, screw drivers, adjustable (monkey) wrench, small assortment of nails, bolts and screws.

Protector: Practice using your own self defense protection device (pepper spray, gun, etc.).

Provisioner: Start learning and practicing some basic meals that you can quickly cook.

Priest: Find and start attending an evangelical Bible preaching church.

Continue a little more each week on your priorities until you are satisfied that your ark is finished or that you are at least initially prepared for the coming flood!

Pre-crisis job skills: Determine what other job skills or income sources you can utilize in a crisis season.

Appendix C: GEAR – for Home or Small Support Group (Tribe)

1. Water filtration system (see water purification main book)
2. Re-chargeable batteries & charger (standard and solar)
3. Additional first-aid supplies (covered in MEDICAL appendix) and your medications   4. Hand Tools (MECHANIC appendix)
5. Wood Splitting Tools (bow saw, axe, splitting wedges); If you are very wood dependent then possibly a chain saw (bar and chain oil, spare chain, chain sharpening file, oil mixture for gas) and/or powered wood splitter)
6. Lanterns (battery, oil or propane powered), plus additional candles and matches
7. If very fortunate, a generator (solar, gas, diesel, propane)
8. Communication gear (see communication in main report)
9. Cooking equipment ("seasoned" cast iron skillet and Dutch oven – works well over open fire), grill and fuel (see Fuel Appendix), aluminum foil, utensils/dishes for the Tribe (including paper plates/bowls, paper towels, dish soap, etc.)
10. Additional personal hygiene items (toilet paper, wet wipes, feminine hygiene products, tooth paste, tooth brushes & floss, deodorant, solar shower bag, towels, wash clothes, soap, etc.)
11. Trash bags (light & heavy duty)   12. Disinfectants (bleach, Lysol)   13. Powdered lime, 5-Gallon buckets with lids and toilet seat for the bucket   14. More mosquito repellant and sunscreen
15. Pet supplies   16. Baby care supplies
17. Reserve copy *Finish Your Ark Now: Prudent Prepper's Primer!*
18. Additional cold weather gear (heavy coat, gloves and mittens that fit over them, wool scarf, wool hat, possibly snow pants or coveralls, wool socks, cold weather waterproof boots)
19. Fire extinguisher(s);   20. Sturdy work clothes (heavy denim pants, web belt, work shirts, cotton/wool socks, boots/shoes)
21. Fuels and some bricks for a "rocket stove"   22. Duct tape
23. Radio (battery AM/FM/shortwave); 24. Mechanical can opener
25. Sewing kit set   26. Glow light sticks (disposable or reusable)

27. Plastic waterproof sheeting   28. Paper with pens/pencils

29. Solar or hand crank phone charger

30. Bicycle or other alternate transportation

31. Tire care: (slime tire sealant, car tire plugs, bicycle tube

repair   32. Other items?

Appendix D: Prep on a Budget

In Mathew 25 – Jesus gives the parable of the five wise and five foolish virgins. All were good people and had the potential opportunity to serve the Master and in turn be blessed. The wise had prepared in advance, but the foolish were not prepared at the unanticipated time of need. The wise could not help them, and were not rebuked by the Master, but the foolish suffered loss because they were not prepared at the right time.

After reading the "Twelve Reasons NOT to Prep" – you may feel a confirmation in your spirit of the need to prep now! The Prepare Now Appendices told you what items to consider for your physical prep as well as necessary skills. Given your present motivation and knowledge, what you need now is to make time and apply resources. If funds are your reason for not prepping then consider the following:

God – Prepping may be as much of a spiritual and emotional issue as a physical issue. Read Psalm 91: 14-16 and write out your responsibilities & God's responses in turn. God is Jehovah-Jireh, but He usually requires us to work for our daily bread as well as pray for it (He is both the God of the supernatural and the natural at the same time).

Gear – What do you already have, what can you get inexpensively (garage sales, Craig's List, etc.) and what can you find on sale? (See Prepare Now Appendix lists).

Grub – Ask neighbors/friends to save you their screw-top liter plastic bottles/glass bottles and fill these with water storage (no cost). Plant a garden/fruit trees (even in small containers), or better yet share-crop with a friend/neighbor/community garden (no dollar cost in return for your labor). Shop for value in canned goods, bulk beans/rice, etc.– food with long storage life. "Buy what you eat and eat what you buy". See if you qualify for food stamps, the food bank or other food assistance programs as this is not a time to let pride stand in your way of preparedness. Grocery shelves empty in 3 days!

Greenbacks – Have some cash safely stored at home for emergency use. Reprioritize your spending habits. Additionally, you can store barter items that would stretch your cash (canned goods, toilet paper, bullets, etc.). Get cash by selling any unneeded items and/or get an additional part-time job or even start a small business on the side. Consider learning new skills (self-taught by internet, library books, taking a class or apprentice with a mentor) which should be useful in any crisis, crashed economy/super decline. Successful employees have good attitudes, usually health-fitness and faith.

Guard Dog – Thieves don't like noise makers (even a recording of a dog barking). Some may prefer other sounds that thieves don't like to hear (ready shot-gun pump)

Everyone needs a plan and can do something to be part of the solution vs. part of the problem (w/out resources in an emergency). **Preparedness is the response of faith!**

Appendix E: GRUB (and water) Food Storage Options

1. <u>Dry</u> items such as powdered milk, cocoa, powdered drink mixes, baking supplies (baking powder, baking soda, yeast, etc.), dried fruits & nuts, milk, sugar, flour or noodles?, various beans, grains – buy bulk and store in food grade plastic buckets (pop-corn, rice, wheat)

2. <u>Canned/jar/foil pouch</u> items such as fish (tuna, salmon, etc.), meat (chicken, beef, beef jerky, hash, pork, smoked meats), <u>lots</u> of peanut butter, jams/jellies, honey, fruit, milk (shelf stable and condensed), various vegetables, soups & stews, flavorings (vanilla, almond extract, etc.), some like MREs (meals ready to eat) - I choose Lara bars, Snickers bars, etc.

3. <u>Freeze-dried or dehydrated</u> items - just add water and cook

4. <u>Bottled</u> items such as water, juice, vinegar (food preservation) and grain alcohol (for medicines and tinctures)

5. <u>Frozen</u> items such as fish, meat, fruit, vegetables, prepared entrees (but consider them a loss if you lose power in a freezer > 2 days or a refrigerator 8-hour time (if you <u>don't open the door!</u>).

6. <u>Spices</u> (especially salt – for cooking and preserving), pepper, and condiments (BBQ sauce, ketchup, mustard, etc.)

7. <u>Fats/oils</u> such as cooking oil, lard, maybe powdered butter?

8. <u>Comfort foods</u> (chocolate, candy, nuts and seeds, cocoa, coffee, tea, etc.

Appendix F: GOD-relationship (personal application)

What follows is what I believe to be the basic building blocks of getting to know God in a personal relationship. Why would the creator of the universe be interested in a relationship with a mere man or woman? Man was created in God's image and God physically walked with Adam and Eve in the Garden.

1 John 4:10 says: "This is love: not that we loved God, but that he loved us and sent his Son (Jesus) as an atoning (acceptable substitute) sacrifice for our sins." Our sin (an archer's term for "missing the mark") separates us from a Holy God. Romans 3:23 says "for all have sinned and fall short of the glory of God." Picture this as a chasm that religion tries to bridge, but fails. Jesus is the only bridge to connect us back to God. "But now in Christ Jesus you who once were far off have been brought near by the blood of Christ" (Ephesians 2:13). "He who has the Son has life; he who does not have the Son of God does not have life" (1 John 5:12). One final scripture is John 3:17 "For God did not send His Son (Jesus) into the world to condemn the world, but that the world through Him might be saved."

The blessings of God are not self executing, so how do you accept this free gift? You must personally reach out and accept it – just like any other gift that is offered to you. Ephesians 2:8 says "For by grace (God's enabling power) you have been saved through faith, and that not of yourselves; it is the gift of God." Romans 10:9 says "that if you confess with your mouth the Lord Jesus and believe in your heart that God has raised Him from the dead, you will be saved." Translation - say it with your words and believe it in your soul (mind, will and emotions). So I take myself off the throne of my life and put Jesus in as the supreme boss - to do what He says and act as He directs (He is the wise creator).

If you have asked Jesus to be King in your life then you are now in covenant (think good marriage) relationship with Him. That means I give all of me (body, mind and spirit) and He in turns gives me all He possess according to His attributes and names. It will take you quite some time to study out the Bible names of Jesus, but you will be blessed in doing this. Our short list of four items is that He has now become your protector, provider, high priest and healer (my chart on the names of Jesus says that there are yet 44 additional names)!

A final thought is how do you get to know and trust a new friend so that in time they become a best friend? Number one is that you spend time with them and learn everything you can about them (this is reading your Bible and attending a church fellowship of other "followers of Jesus". Yes, the Bible says "not forsaking the assembling of ourselves together, as is the manner of some, but exhorting one another, and so much the more as you see the Day approaching" (Hebrews 10:25). The Christian life is lived in relationship, both with God and with people.

Number two, is that you talk with your new friend daily (this is prayer – it starts with dear Jesus, includes "saying thank you God" as well as asking for His help, and ends with "Amen – so be it Lord"). Communication is a two-way street, so also take time to be quiet and listen as you ask Him to speak to your spirit. Jeremiah 33:3 says: 'Call to Me (Jesus), and I will answer you, and show you great and mighty things, which you do not know.'

Number three, is that you don't let anything get in the way of your primary relationship with Jesus. While we are told to reach the world with His good news message, we don't enter into any relationships (marital, personal, business partnerships, etc.) that divide our loyalty to Christ. 2 Corinthians 6:14-18 says: "Do not be unequally yoked together with unbelievers. For what fellowship has righteousness with lawlessness? ...And what communion has light with darkness? For you are the temple of the living God." As God has said: "'I will dwell in them And walk among them. I will be their God, And they shall be My people. Therefore Come out from among them And be separate, says the Lord. ...And I will receive you. I will be a Father to you, And you shall be My sons and daughters, Says the Lord Almighty.'"

Appendix G: Master Gardener Tools and Equipment

You may be able to find some of this as used equipment at auctions, farm sales, garage sales, etc. Most of the bigger items can be rented if only needed for infrequent use.

*Hand tools (shovels, rakes, hoes, pitch forks, pry bars, chains, brooms, pick axes, manual post-hole diggers, etc.)

*Gardening tools (hand trowel, hand-claw, watering can, hand pruners, garden scissors, loppers, ground stakes, garden hose, sprayer-head)

*Trellis materials (tomato cages, hog panels, etc.)

*Seed starting supplies (small cups with bottom holes, trays w/out holes, containers for planting, potting soil, mulch

*Raised garden beds (also 1/2 – inch PVC pipe for hoops, freeze cloth

*lots of plastic buckets and crates   *hoses and funnels

*wheel barrows, wagons, and dolly

*come-along hand-operated winch and wire stretcher

*ATVs (all-terrain vehicles or 4 -wheelers) and pick-up trucks

*flatbed trailer and enclosed animal trailer   *zero-turn mower

*tractors and their equipment attachments: brush-hog, posthole digger, lift bucket, cultivator, box-end scraper or blade, etc.

*sprayers (one for herbicides and a second one for pesticides),

Appendix H: Medical Kit Lists

I have three different first-aid kits that I have assembled depending on where I am going and my expected support role.

1. My personal first-aid carry is a 3.5"x3.5"x1.75" canvas belt pouch. It contains: CPR shield, rubber gloves, BZK antiseptic wipe, 2 aspirin, magnifying glass, tweezers, small compass, magnesium fire start stick, 2 safety pins, whistle, LED light, 2 water purification tablets, band-aids, cough drops and a small pocket knife.

2. My second first-aid carry is a large fanny pack when I am responsible for a small group. Similar to the belt pouch first-aid kit it contains everything from the belt pouch plus: mask, bandage scissors, reflective survival blanket, triangle bandage, CAT (combat application tourniquet), 1 roll of coban adhesive wrap, small notepad, pencil/pen, lighter, "H"-pressure bandage, sun glasses, chest seals, irrigation syringe, stethoscope (cheap), room thermometer, soap, dental floss, Claritan & Pepcid (can be taken together as mild allergic reaction meds). If you have severe allergies, and have been prescribed an EpiPen (epinephrine treatment for anaphylactic shock/reaction), then keep it with you, honey (blood sugar boost), hand sanitizer, albuterol inhaler (personal use), wound kit [compressed gauze, steri-strips, tincture of benzoin (adhesive for strips), anti-biotic ointment, duct tape, cloth tape, 3x3 gauze pads, finger size SAM splint], flashlight/lite-stick, and a small first-aid guide.

3. I also have an EMT-size seven pouch medical bag, because in addition to being part of the Medical skills group (I have training as an EMR) we also have some ER nurses in our Tribe. Therefore, we might function as Medical for a nearby Tribe that has less Medical skill (Community concept). Items in this

Appendix H (con't.): Medical Kit Lists

medical trauma bag: flashlight; 2 reflective survival wrap blanket/sheets; 2 CPR masks (child and adult); 2 tourniquets; small notepad; sharpie pen and pencil; 2 rolls 2-inch cloth tape; 2 rolls coban wrap; roll ½-inch transpore tape; roll ½-inch cloth tape; 20 4x4 gauze pads; steri-strips (wound closure); benzion tincture (adhesive for steri-strips); band-aids & specialty band-aids; pulse-oxygen meter; medical gloves; surgical mask; water pure tablets; tweezers; shave razor; super glue; soap; 10 big safety pins; 4 elastic wraps; aspirin (325 mg); Naproxen (pain relief);   Claritan (aka Loratadine) and Pepcid (aka Famotidine) - taken together as allergic reaction meds; 2 hemostats (clamps); 4 "H"- compression bandages; partial roll of Saran wrap; alcohol pads; cotton cleansing pads; antibiotic packets, bite-sting kit; good stethoscope; BP (blood pressure) device (sygmomanometer); BVM (bag valve mask); wound stapler & staple puller; goggles; oral airway (2 sizes); bandage scissors; thermometer (temple touch); 2 irrigation syringes; cake icing tubes (diabetic treatment); 3 nasal trumpets with lube; BZK antiseptic; instant ice bags; pulse-ox meter; small medical book (A Comprehensive Guide to Wilderness and Travel Medicine - Eric Weiss, MD; ISBN 0-9659768-1-5).

Note: if you are planning on just one medical reference guide then get the Weiss pocket book. Other non-professional medical references are "Where There Is No Dentist" by Dickson (ISBN:0-942364-05-8) and "Where There Is No Doctor: a village health care handbook" by Werner (ISBN:0-942364-15-5).

Also review Appendix I: Common Medical Conditions and Treatments

<u>**Appendix I: Common Medical Conditions & Potential Treatments**</u>

<u>**Disclaimer:**</u> **We are not diagnosing any disease or medical condition, nor are we providing you with treatment directives - as that is something that only you and your healthcare provider can decide. We are simply sharing educational information and some of our own personal experiences and tips that were helpful to us. If you are unsure of any of the terms listed then get medical help as necessary. The list below is a quick summary overview intended for wilderness emergencies and in consultation with a healthcare provider. General Safety Guidelines for any service provider: wear rubber gloves & glasses/goggles to protect yourself from other bodily fluids & germs. Observe and make sure the area is safe before entering.**

<u>**Chronic and Severe Medical Conditions**</u> **(discuss with physician now!) As we face the prospect of uncertain times, we must consider the possibility that medical care as we now know it in America may become less reliable. If you have more complicated medical needs, what can you do to prepare? You probably already know much about your condition, but learn and understand as completely as you possibly can. Knowledge is Power! Obtain printed materials that can be referred to later by you and your care team if the internet is unavailable. Increase your wellness to the best you can possibly achieve now. Adhere strictly to your disease maintenance regimen to make the most of the health you do have. Most of us fall into a complacent "path of least resistance" when we deal with something long term. But being at your maximum wellness level will give you more resilience when healthcare is intermittently reliable. Now is the time to take the advice your healthcare provider has been suggesting all along: walk more, take your meds routinely, gain weight or lose weight, do your exercises, etc. Perhaps you can stock up on supplies you use. Perhaps you can reorder routine medications as soon as possible to build up a small surplus. (Consider the best storage conditions to prolong the life of your current supply.)**

Discuss your options with your healthcare provider for how to prepare for potential supply chain breakdowns. Ask how your condition is treated in less advanced countries. There are important things you can do to prepare now!

Section 1: Physiological Shock

Shock is the body's response to a physical trauma. If shock continues to progress, the body begins shutting down and eventually restricts blood flow to the vital organs and cells causing death. Shock may be caused by excessive blood loss, poisoning, burns, heart failure, blood infections, dehydration and severe allergic reactions. Symptoms of shock include rapid heart rate, low blood pressure and weak pulse.

<u>Treatment for shock</u> - have the person lie down with the feet elevated 12-inches, keep them warm and call for medical help. If the head or chest is injured or they are having trouble breathing, elevate the upper body instead. Always treat for shock if someone has experienced a significant traumatic injury. If possible, resolve the situation causing shock, if not get emergency help!

Section 2: Respiratory

Respiratory illnesses have many different causes, but for simplicity we will divide them into viral, bacterial and chronic conditions. We will deal with the most common and easily treated at home conditions and leave the more acute conditions to others.

The most common is the average cold which attacks the upper airway (nose, throat, and sinus.) Flu is a cousin virus which is more severe and may additionally affect the lower respiratory tract (lungs). Both are virus types, are short lived, self limiting and likely unaffected by antibiotics. Sometimes the body is weakened by a virus and then invaded by bacteria. Examples of this are a cold that turns into a bacterial sinus or ear infection or a flu virus that becomes bacterial pneumonia. A cold or flu that was improving, and then becomes severe again with rising temperatures or mucus that thickens and changes color is suspicious of bacteria and needs evaluation for recommended antibiotics. (Bacterial infections may be entirely unrelated to a virus as well.) Even though these have different causes, the home care and control of symptoms are very similar. See the chart below for comparisons.

COLD SYMPTOMS	FLU DIFFERENCES
Sneezy, runny, stuffy nose nasal discharge	Less likely to sneeze
Starts slowly, lower temp (<100), <u>headache, mild body aches</u>	Rapid high temperature (>100), more aches/pains, worse headache
General fatigue	Severe exhaustion
Usually just upper respiratory tract (nose, throat + sinus)	Involves upper + lower respiratory tract (lungs) + more likely to cause pneumonia
Vit C, D3, Zinc + E may prevent or decrease length of cold and flu	Take Vitamins C, D3, Zinc & E Antiviral drugs avail esp 1st 48hrs may shorten or decrease severity
Incubation 1-3 days (time between exposure and symptoms when we are also contagious)	Incubation 1-4 days (contagious)
Sick up to a week	Sick up to 2 weeks; COVID flu type?

During cold and flu season taking vitamin C, D3 and E may help prevent catching or decrease the severity of colds and flu. Consider taking label recommended dosage for maintenance and prevention. If we get sick we take 500mg of Vitamin C two or more times a day, we take 1,000 up to 4,000 IU of Vitamin D3 once a day, 200 IU of Vitamin E once a day and Zinc 8mg but no more than 40mg a day (long term or excessive use may be harmful.) Zinc taken in the nose could potentially cause damage to the sense of smell, but throat lozenges are effective in shortening the length of the common cold.

Treatments for colds and flu: involve abundant rest, fluids and things that soothe the respiratory tract. Warm fluids like chicken soup, bone broth, hot tea with lemon and honey, provide fluid and soothe the throat (and may have curative properties of their own.) Warm salt water gargle soothes a sore throat. Saline flushes may ease sinus pain and pressure and may prevent sinus infection. Saline can be made by adding 1 teaspoon of salt to 2 cups of boiling water and cool to lukewarm before use. Breathing steamy water (like hot shower, breathing the steam from a simmering pot of soup or having a vaporizer in the room) adds moisture to keep mucus thin and decrease congestion.

Dehydration (lack of moisture) thickens mucus... DRINK LOTS of water! If you have thick mucus that you can't cough up, you might try Mucinex (guaifenesin) in concentrated pill form or as an ingredient in cough syrup. Again, the body needs enough fluid to thin the mucus. Menthol in a vapor or a cough drop can be very helpful in calming a cough. "Fisherman's Friend" is a brand of very strong menthol cough drop that we find effective. Vitamin C / Zinc lozenges provide vitamins as well as soothe the throat. Uncontrolled coughing creates a vicious cycle of rapidly worsening cough and should be addressed.

Asthma is a chronic condition that affects approximately 25 million in the U.S. or 8% of the population. During an attack it causes the airways to narrow and swell and produce extra mucus. This can make breathing difficult and trigger coughing, a whistling sound called wheezing when you breathe out, and shortness of breath. This can be a minor inconvenience or a life threatening event and is most quickly treated medically with drugs like albuterol inhalers (among others.) Difficulty breathing is very frightening and unfortunately anxiety increases the symptoms. So speaking calmly and soothing the person having the attack while waiting for their meds to work can be helpful. Resting with head and chest elevated and perhaps raising arms to shoulder height may decrease the effort of breathing. If you have asthma be sure to keep plenty of your medication on hand, it may not be easy to get in an emergency! There are natural remedies that can complement medication, but probably can't adequately substitute, so never run out! Consistent, asthma specific, exercise training and breathing exercises may improve lung function and improve overall health. Turmeric and magnesium have shown some benefits as have massage and relaxation therapy. Warm showers and hot drinks may relax the throat. Perhaps these disciplines will decrease, but not replace, the amount of medication required for treating this dangerous condition.

Choking: If the person is speaking or coughing let them try to remove the problem themself, but do not leave them. If they have an obstructed airway they usually will exhibit the universal sign of choking, holding the neck with their hands and having the look of panic or confusion on their face. Have someone call 911 for help and then begin the Heimlich maneuver: from behind, reach around the person, place fist with thumb against the belly button, grab the fist with your other hand and quickly pull into the belly, HARD. Alternately for a pregnant or large abdomen person give chest thrusts: put your fist on the breastbone, grab fist with other hand and pull quick and hard (like the Heimlich.) Repeat one of these until the blockage is removed or they pass out. If this happens, lower the person onto the floor face up, arms to their sides. Clear the airway by opening the mouth, and if you can see the object, reach a finger in to sweep out the object. Do not sweep what you cannot see, especially in young children as you risk pushing the blockage deeper. If the person becomes unconscious, begin CPR with chest compressions and rescue breaths. To prepare yourself for these situations, learn the Heimlich maneuver and CPR in a certified first aide training class (this training is even available online).

Unable to breathe: Can be caused by a fall or being hit in the stomach. This is caused by a spasm of the diaphragm. This is a self-resolving condition. In the meantime go into the curled fetal position and try to relax, knowing that it will soon pass and you will again be breathing. A laryngospasm is similar, but is a transient and reversible spasm of the vocal cords that makes it difficult to speak or breathe. It can have different causes such as getting choked by the water while swimming, acid reflux or even extreme fear. The breathing difficulty can be alarming, but it's not life-threatening. If it happens, try to relax, it will pass soon.

Section 3: Fever

Fever is the body's signal that something is wrong and we should pay attention. Sometimes fever accompanies a chronic condition. An example would be Rheumatoid Arthritis which causes inflammation which elevates temperature. When the body is overheated as in dehydration in a high temperature environment the body responds with fever. (see section on heat stroke)

But usually fever is the result of an infection. We generally regard fever as our body's friend during illness or infection and unless it's excessive (over 104) we tolerate it to help our body heal itself. Fever works in 2 ways; first because virus and bacteria thrive in lower body temperatures, fevers may weaken, kill or prevent a virus from reproducing which helps stop the virus in its tracks! Secondly, fever stimulates the immune system to produce more white cells and other disease fighters and to make them more active in their job to fight off disease. Yes, fever can increase body aches and headaches, but before you reach for the Tylenol or NSAIDs (aspirin, ibuprofen or naproxen) try less clothing, a cool washcloth, or lukewarm bath. That will decrease fever, but not eliminate the healing properties of the fever allowing your body to heal faster! Studies have shown that NSAIDS can decrease the activity of the white blood cells (germ fighters) by 50% - Not good! OK, but don't fevers cause seizures? Not usually unless over 104 degrees. And, according to the Mayo Clinic, "Seizures are usually harmless, only last a few minutes and typically don't indicate a serious health problem." (mayoclinic.org/diseases- conditions/febrileseizure). Indications of a more serious problem include severe vomiting, stiff neck, breathing problems and difficulty waking. Giving Tylenol or NSAIDS at the beginning of a fever will not prevent a seizure according to the Mayo Clinic website.

Some exceptions to not treating a fever: infants under 3 months of age, any child with a fever over 104, a feverish child who won't wake up easily, a feverish child with a stiff neck and pain when touched, a child who has a seizure disorder. These children need to see your doctor or even a timelier ER visit.

Section 4: Gastro-Intestinal Illnesses:

Nausea/Vomiting/Diarrhea (N/V/D) can be caused by viruses, bacteria, parasites, ingesting poisons and certain medical conditions.   See the chart below for comparisons.

VIRUS	BACTERIA	FOOD POISONING	PARASITES
An infectious microbe that takes over a host cell	Like E-Coli or Salmonella	Infectious organisms or their toxins in spoiled food	Like malaria fr mosquitoes or worms from pets
Stomach flu onset 12 – 48 hours after exposure	Onset 1 – 14 days after exposure	Rapid onset 30 minutes to 4 hours after eating	May have no symptoms, may take months or yrs
Virus last 1-3 days	May last weeks or more	Most less than 24 hrs, self limiting, treat diet/rest	Infection cured w/ meds. Effects may be years

VIRUS	BACTERIA	FOOD POISONING	PARASITES
Very contagious , but spread over few days	Stool culture to determine organism	All who ate get sick about the same time	More common in countries w/ mosquitoes
Self limiting	Carried in human feces & by poultry and reptiles	Spoiled food, poor hand washing, unclean surfaces	More common in poorer countries

Food poisoning is the most rapid onset and is usually quickly resolved. The main indication that it is food related is that it starts 30 minutes to a few hours after ingesting bad food. Other people who have eaten the bad food will also become ill at the same time. The body will get rid of the toxins quickly, so vomiting and diarrhea may be rapid and unavoidable. However, usually a few times will be the worst of it! Do not try to stop the process with drugs; the body is protecting you from food poisoning! If you've eaten bad food at home, the food should be destroyed and the kitchen and utensils sanitized. If it was consumed elsewhere, the location (and perhaps the health department for commercial kitchens) should be notified so they can do the same and perhaps limit the number of people affected!

Food is not the only source of bacteria. Hand washing after using the bathroom (or facilities) and before eating is a routine health precaution for this reason. Live poultry are notorious for carrying E-coli and salmonella. Children especially need to be instructed not to cuddle or nuzzle chickens and to wash thoroughly after handling poultry or their eggs or doing routine chores. Fresh poultry meat has salmonella on its surface; rinse meat before cutting, wash tools and surfaces thoroughly before preparing other foods, wash hands well between meats and produce. Pet reptiles, including wild toads, frogs, turtles and snakes also carry these bacteria! Parents, educate your children on their safe handling.

<u>Stomach virus:</u> (frequently called the stomach flu) is different from food poisoning. It usually takes 12 - 48 hours after exposure to someone with the flu for symptoms to appear. It is very contagious, so other people will also come down with it, but not simultaneously like food poisoning. The virus is transmitted orally and through mucous membranes or breaks in the skin. Containment will be focused on handwashing and sanitation for all people and semi-isolation for the sick. Routinely clean kitchen/dining surfaces and commonly touched areas like faucets, toilets, doorknobs and handrails with a disinfecting solution. Teach all ages to keep their hands off their face and eyes and not put anything except food (and special teething toys for babies) in their mouths. Wash children's toys often if they haven't learned this yet! A stomach virus is not treated with antibiotics and usually lasts 1-3 days. Full recovery takes a little longer.

<u>Treatment of N/V/D:</u> is primarily concerned with maintaining hydration while allowing the gut to rest before gradually re-introducing gentle foods. This requires time and patience!

Because stimulating the stomach (gastric system) makes the symptoms worse, all food at this point should be avoided. Fluids should be frequent but very gradual. Think teaspoonfuls every 15 minutes! Plain water is less well tolerated than an <u>ORS - oral rehydration solution</u> (because the molarity of water is different than the fluid in the stomach). ORS contains three things: clean water, electrolytes and carbohydrates. The simplest emergency ORS to make would be a pinch of salt and a teaspoon of sugar in a cup of room temperature water. Alternatively, coconut water contains electrolytes and would be better with a splash of apple juice for carbohydrates. Or DIY ginger tea made with a slice of fresh ginger, honey and hot water. Weakened broth contains salt and a little carbohydrate (avoid too much salt). Sport drinks cut with half water or children's pedialyte solution are an option as well. Emetrol is a natural solution, available over the counter that some people swear by. It is important to follow all directions exactly for best results. As the N/V/D subside, gradually increase the volume and frequency of the ORS. Water and clear jello may be added.

Foods to avoid during recovery: caffeinated or alcoholic beverages, avoid high fat, high sugar and excessive salt, avoid carbonated drinks, avoid dairy (except nursing babies should continue breast milk.) For the first 2-3 days do not take medication like Imodium to stop diarrhea; the body is trying to heal itself of toxins and will recover faster if given the chance. After 2-3 days, an anti-diarrhea or anti-nausea med may be helpful. But usually the cause for continued symptoms is that the gut wasn't allowed to rest long enough before reintroducing foods. The next day start the B.R.A.T. diet (stands for bananas, rice, applesauce and toast.) This would also include white crackers, white noodles in broth, apple juice and cooked white rice cereal. The next day, begin soft foods like poached eggs, well cooked veggies, lean chicken, canned fruit, baked or boiled potato, chicken noodle or vegetable soup. Avoid milk, dairy, greasy or spicy foods, raw veggies, and whole grains. Fiber from raw produce and whole grains is very healthy under normal circumstances. But it is hard to digest, and we are resting the gut! Continue to avoid alcohol, caffeine and carbonation. By the 4th day you should be back on your normal diet. Severe N/V/D that lasts longer than 24 hours in a child or 3 days for an adult without improving (if you have followed the previous instructions) may indicate something more serious and you should contact your doctor. Staying hydrated cannot be overemphasized!

Dehydration: Mild dehydration is common and easily treated (see oral rehydration solution above) but severe dehydration is life threatening, especially in infants. Symptoms for an infant or very young child include: visibly dry mouth and tongue, no tears when crying, no wet diapers for over 3 hours, sunken eyes and cheeks, sunken soft spot on top of their head (fontanels) and being irritable and without energy. Adults: extreme thirst (also lack of thirst), less frequent urination, dark urine, fatigue, dizziness, confusion, fever, lack of sweat and rapid pulse. When it gets to this point it is difficult to treat without IVs (fluids in the vein), so practice good hydration!

Constipation: may cause N/V/D especially in the elderly, infants, those on narcotics or otherwise infirm. This is why they always monitor the frequency of bowel movements in the hospital and nursing homes. This group of people may not be able to remember or report this issue. Constipation is a very common cause for emergency room visits or even cause for emergency surgery. It is often easily treated in the early stages: think prunes, glycerin suppositories, enemas! It is not so easy when advanced. Often drinking more water or improving the diet (including more fiber) while well can prevent constipation in a normal digestive system. For some medical conditions, chronic pain requiring narcotics and some bowel dysfunctions, constipation is simply something that has to be managed. Medical help is advised.

Section 5: Urinary Tract Infections (urethra, bladder, ureters or kidneys). Most involve the urethra and bladder and are more common in women. Serious health problems can result if it spreads to the kidneys. Common symptoms with urinating are urgency, burning, frequency, incontinence and spasm after voiding. Cloudy, bloody or foul odor of urine, pelvic pain and pressure are additional symptoms. Infection of the urethra can cause a discharge. A more serious kidney infection is indicated by back or side pain, high fever, chills and nausea and vomiting. UTI's can be caused by E Coli - which is found in the gut. Prevent this contaminant by wiping front to back, perineal hygiene and voiding after sexual activity. Concentrated urine grows more bacteria, so stay hydrated. Regular intake of vitamin C or cranberry juice is a helpful preventative and treatment. Some risk factors: irritating chemicals found in feminine hygiene products, hormonal changes after menopause, enlarged prostate, suppressed immune system and diabetes.

<u>Treatments for UTI:</u> immediately begin drinking more water and taking more vitamin C. Visit your doctor who will order a urine culture to see which organism is responsible, which helps determine the best antibiotic. Common drugs are Bactrim, Bactrim DS, Cephalaxin, and Nitrofurantoin. Usually symptoms clear in a few days, but you must complete your medication to prevent recurrence. For immediate pain relief, you may take an OTC drug called <u>Pyridium (Phenazopyridine)</u> or Azo. This is for pain relief only and does not deal with the infection, so an antibiotic is still needed! Kidney infections left untreated can cause kidney damage which can result in kidney failure.

Section 6: Cardio-Vascular

<u>Heart Attack Symptoms:</u> Chest pain, pressure, tightness or aching sensation in the center of the chest. It also can be pain or discomfort that spreads to the shoulder, arm, back, neck, teeth, or occasionally upper abdomen. Additionally can be nausea, indigestion or heartburn, sometimes vomiting, shortness of breath, lightheadedness, dizziness, fainting and sweating. A heart attack generally causes chest pain for more than 15 minutes; some have mild pain while in others it is more severe. Women tend to have more vague symptoms and are more difficult to diagnose. Do not "wait to be sure" – consider it's a heart attack and call 911 or have someone drive you. Chew and swallow an aspirin unless you are allergic to aspirin. (chewing helps it absorb in the mouth faster). If you have been previously prescribed nitroglycerin, take it as directed. If the person becomes unconscious or was found that way to begin with, check for pulse and breathing (in absence, start CPR). If an AED (automated external defibrillator) is available and the person is unconscious, follow the device instructions.

<u>Stroke:</u> Occurs when there's bleeding in the brain or when brain blood flow is blocked. In this second case, it could be compared to a heart attack, but occurring in the brain.

Symptoms: F.A.S.T

<u>Face</u> droop on one side when person tries to smile.

<u>Arms,</u> one arm is weaker or hangs lower when told to raise them.

<u>Speech</u>. Can a person answer a simple question, is speech slurred?

<u>Time.</u> During a stroke every minute counts, call 911 and get them to the hospital. Some strokes can be reversed if treated in time.

Aspirin should never be taken for a stroke because if it is caused by bleeding, the aspirin can make bleeding worse. You won't know which it is until scans are taken at the hospital. Don't delay, just get them there F.A.S.T!

Section 7: Environmental Hazards

<u>Frostbite:</u> Excessive cooling of the skin (particularly the fingers, toes, nose and ears) due to exposed skin or inadequate clothing in cold temperatures, wind and wet. Symptoms are pain, red to white blanched color and numbness. Frost nip is the early stage and frost burn is the more severe condition (fracturing of cells). Prevention is proper clothing and getting out of the wind/wet. Treatment is gentle warming – especially skin to skin (hands in armpits or I once put my brothers' feet on my bare stomach!). Drink warm liquids, but don't drink alcohol. Don't re-warm with direct heat; your body may not sense something being too hot and cause a burn. With a severe frostbite you may see blisters form. Do not break them!

<u>Hypothermia:</u> Is a medical emergency where core body temperature drops below 95-degrees (normal temperature is 98.6) due to exposure to cold temperatures (including wind or immersion in cold water.) Mild symptoms are shivering, mental confusion, unclear speech, high heart and breathing rates; moderate symptoms (core temp of 82-90) are no shivering, dilated pupils and increased confusion; severe symptoms (core temp < 82) can include hallucinations, undressing in the cold, non-reactive pupils (no reaction to light shined in the eyes), labored breathing, fluid buildup

in lungs, heart attack and unconsciousness. Treatment is to remove any wet clothing in a warm and dry setting, cover with blankets, skin to skin contact with another person and sips of a warm drink (not alcohol and only if conscious). Don't rub or massage the person or encourage physical activity. If you must wait for help outdoors, shield them from the cold and especially wind as much as possible, keep them horizontal, cover them up including the head, leaving airspace for breathing, insulate their body from the cold ground.

Dehydration: Dehydration is simply not having enough water to keep the body functioning well. It can occur from excessive sweating, loss of fluids from fever, vomiting or diarrhea, certain medications like diuretics or from simply not drinking enough water. Symptoms of dehydration include thirst (at least one pint low), headache, fatigue, dizziness, dry mouth and urine that is dark yellow. Alcohol and caffeinated drinks (coffee, energy drinks, etc.) actually cause the body to expel water. Sports drinks (Gatorade, etc.) and juices should be cut 50/50 with water to keep from initially pulling water out of the blood stream. Cool, but not cold water, is absorbed faster. Oral rehydrating solutions replace the electrolytes lost in sweat. If possible, move out of the sun to somewhere cool. Water aids all body functions and is essential to human health – drink water (caffeinated drinks and alcohol are dehydrating)!

Heat Illness: Is the collective term for your body's inability to rid itself of a heat load. Heat cramps may be linked with dehydration, (see previous section for treatment) excessive exercise or an overly hot environment. Heat Exhaustion is recognized by nausea, dizziness, excessive sweating, weakness and thirst. Get the person to a cooler environment and sip cool water. If this treatment is ignored, or the heat load increases, then life threatening Heat Stroke can occur. Dizziness gets worse, sweating stops, mental confusion takes over and eventually a person may lose consciousness. This is a medical emergency that requires getting the core body temperature down (cooler environment; ice packs at neck, groin and armpits; remove excess clothing). Get medical help!

Section 8: Major Trauma

<u>Head Injury:</u> A motor vehicle accident, a blow to the head or a fall may jolt the brain to internally hit the skull and result in a brain bruise or brain bleed. A blow to the head has also affected the neck; avoid moving the neck and do not remove a helmet. A mild concussion can have minor symptoms like headache or dizziness, but have major problems that appear later. Treatment is rest under observation – especially the first 12-24 hours, but could be as long as 3 days. Get medical treatment if symptoms worsen. Severe symptoms can include loss of consciousness, dilated pupils, unequal pupil size, severe nausea and vomiting, headache, slurred speech, trouble walking, and confusion. They may be very sleepy and difficult to waken. This person may seem oriented, but lack the judgment to know they are injured. They need medical intervention. If the brain continues to bleed internally, it will cause pressure that could result in brain damage. Broken skin on the head and face bleeds a lot; cover a wound with absorbent padding and hold pressure. If you suspect a fractured skull do not use pressure.

<u>Gun Shot Wound:</u> When there has been a shooting, call 911 first. Then check the situation; is there an active shooter or ongoing violence? If possible ensure that you and the victim are in a safe place or at least behind cover. Look for blood, then trace it back to find the gunshot wound. The first thing to do is stop the bleeding by applying pressure directly over the wound. Wad up towels or clothing to add absorbent pressure. If the wound is large you may be able to pack the wound with sterile gauze or even a tampon. Pushing this into the wound with the fingers will hurt, but will help. Do not delay putting direct pressure to the site by looking for supplies. Do not release pressure! The person should be lying down, but do not elevate their legs. While waiting, begin gathering medical information: name, contact persons, allergies to meds, current medications, and important medical conditions. This info will help emergency professionals to give needed care. If the patient loses consciousness, it will be too late to obtain his info! If no ambulance is coming, use medical professionals.

Crush Injuries: Crush injuries of the torso have the potential of broken ribs or spine and internal bleeding or punctured lungs, and need immediate medical help. Call 911! Avoid moving the person without stabilizing the spine. Despite this, if they are pulse-less and not breathing, begin CPR!

For crush injuries that appear to be surface on the extremities; control bleeding, control swelling and pain (elevate body part, bandage, ice – 15 minutes on and 15 minutes off). Patient needs to be medically evaluated for broken bones.

Stabbing or Impalement: I am defining a stab as a wound made with a sharp object which was then withdrawn. Impalement would be a sharp object which is still protruding from the body. With stabbing injuries it is possible to have a small surface cut with deep injuries, so further assessment by a professional is advised. Be aware that a stab to the chest could injure the heart and major arteries, or the lungs and breathing. Either one would be life threatening. A stab to the abdomen could do a lot of damage but is less likely to cause death from bleeding that day.

When an object is sticking out of the body it is best to not remove it. Sometimes the pressure of the object is the only thing preventing massive hemorrhaging. It is not possible to see how deep or into what organ the object has pierced. Therefore, move the person to medical care (or wait for an ambulance) without removing the object. It is probably advisable to use tape to secure the object to the skin. A long object (like an arrow or spear) might be cut to shorten it for transport. If the person is impaled on an immovable object it might be possible to use loppers or a bolt cutter to cut the object next to the ground and then transport.

Broken Bones: All broken bones need medical evaluation. The person will be more comfortable if the injured area is padded and splinted to support the broken bone. An example could be as simple as supporting an arm or ankle with a pillow for a car ride. In remote locations you might pad the same break with a t-shirt and apply sticks for splints and wrap them in place for support so the patient is able to travel. A compound fracture is when the bone has broken thru the skin creating a source of infection. Because the broken bone may have gone back under the skin, any cut over a fracture is suspicious. Bone infections are very serious! Cover the bone or opening in the skin with a sterile dressing to prevent further contamination and get help quickly. Ice and elevation of broken extremities will reduce pain and swelling.

Section 9: Other Medical Conditions

Muscle Soreness: Muscle soreness is expected for athletes, but may be an unpleasant surprise for sedentary people who dramatically increase their physical activity. See the section on Functional Physical Fitness to get ideas for improving wellness. The body's muscles are attached to bone and joints and can develop soreness as a result of physical work. Increasing the temperature and blood flow to muscles before work helps muscles function optimally (like a warm rubber band vs. a rubber band in the freezer). Whole body movement warm-up (walking, gentle calisthenics, etc.) and a cool-down period including some gentle stretching may decrease feelings of soreness. Muscle rubs that make the skin surface feel hot or cold, are not really deep penetrating to the muscles, but can decrease the feeling of muscle discomfort. They trick the body into only accepting the hot or cold sensation while blocking the pain signal from the muscle (you know now the counter-irritant theory of discomfort control). I have personally found that massage of a muscle or acupressure (same principle as acupuncture without the needles) is also effective in treating muscle discomfort.

Muscle Cramps: Are a painful contraction of a muscle (usually arch of foot or calf muscle) that may show up as stabbing muscle pain. Treatment is to stretch that muscle to get it to relax and return to normal tension. Massage the cramped muscle with firm pressure. Muscle cramps can occur due to fatigue of a muscle or to an internal imbalance of electrolytes like calcium, potassium, and magnesium. Severe or frequently recurring muscle cramps can indicate a medical problem, so see your doctor.

Strains and Sprains: Stretch or tear of the ligament (holds bones next to each other together) or a stretch/tear of a tendon (connects bone to a muscle) or a stretch/tear of a muscle is a strain or sprain.

R.I.C.E. it for treatment:
Rest
Ice 15 minutes on/off
Compression (wrap, but check to see that limb pulse is not impacted)
Elevation (body part higher than the heart)

Avoid weight bearing activities and keep it elevated for at least 3 days with a severe ankle sprain (crutches). If the pain is severe or feels unstable when trying to use it, see your doctor. In an emergency, if you must walk out to get additional help, then stabilize joint with a splint and/or sling. Use a walking stick or buddy to help support your weight.

Animal Bites and Puncture Wounds: Initial bleeding is helpful to clear the wound of animal germs and/or dirt. Flush the wound with running water then cover the wound with a sterile bandage treated with antibiotic. Change the dressing daily. The wound must heal from the inside out to the skin surface. Watch for signs of infection (pus or yellow drainage; red, hot and swollen tissue) and get professional help if that occurs. During the early infection phase, soaking the area in very warm water with Epsom salt and/or iodine solution may draw out the infection. If it becomes red, hot and swollen with drainage and especially if you see red streaks from the wound toward the heart it is becoming a serious infection. See a doctor for antibiotics. If the animal bite is unprovoked a wild animal should be shot, if possible, and tested for rabies. A domestic dog or cat may have had a rabies vaccine; they can be taken to the vet to watch for possible rabies.

Bee stings and Spider bites: Are recognized by pain, redness and swelling. Most spider bites are not serious. Bee stings can be minimized by getting the stinger and its venom sac out of the skin immediately. Remove this stinger with a fingernail, credit card or tweezers (wasps don't lose their stinger and can sting repeatedly. All insect bites and stings treatment can proceed by applying ice or some suggest using a baking soda paste. If someone is allergic to bee stings this can be life threatening and they may already carry their epi-pen with them. If not, or if the new sting causes a severe allergic reaction (called anaphylaxis) then get medical help immediately. Symptoms can include throat swelling, shortness of breath, itchy rash, numbness and lightheadedness.

Bleeding: Remove clothing and loose debris from the wound. Do not remove embedded objects or probe the wound. Use a clean towel to apply firm pressure to the area until bleeding stops (this may take a few minutes.) Don't press on an eye injury! Don't press on an embedded object or if you suspect a skull fracture. Add more gauze or cloth if blood is seeping through. Help the person lie down, watch for shock. Progressive order to stop blood loss is; direct pressure to the wound → pressure to the artery above the wound → tourniquet (need training and medical help to apply and especially for release). If tourniquet must be used, note time it is applied to report to emergency help. Some possible dressings include; Band-aids, gauze pads or pressure wrap, steri-strips/butterfly bandages and an "H-wrap" pressure bandage (for severe bleeding.)

Skin Abrasions: Wash the wound with soap and water. Try to remove dirt and foreign material (can use a clean soft toothbrush or gauze pad). Cover with bandage treated with antibiotic. Change daily and watch for signs of infection.

Wound infections: Minor infections are indicated by pain and redness. Wash, treat with antibiotic ointment and a dressing 3 times a day. Redness should go away by day 4 and complete healing by day 10. More severely infected wounds have pain and redness, plus yellowish-green discharge or pus, may have odor, may have red streaks coming from the wound. The wound infection is invading the body and can cause a whole body infection called sepsis. In sepsis the person will develop more body pains, fever, chills and vomiting and may exhibit signs of shock. Sepsis is an emergency that cannot be treated at home.

Burns and Sunburn: First degree burns and sunburns just affect the top layer of skin. Cool the burn, immerse the burn in cool tap water or apply cold wet compresses for about 10 minutes or until pain lessens. Remove rings or other tight items on affected hand. Don't break blisters (second degree burn) as this exposes the burn to infection. Cover the burned area with gauze.

More severe burns are deep, result in dry, leathery skin or charring. They are large or cover the face, hands, feet, buttocks or groin. They may be over a major joint or encircling an arm or a leg. Major burns require emergency medical care. They may result in shock. Remove restrictive items from their body such as belts and jewelry as burned areas typically swell quickly. Cover the burned area with a clean cloth that's moistened with cool clean water. Remove clothing over a burn, but not if it is stuck to the skin. Do not apply any burn ointments or home remedies. Get medical care!

Nosebleed: The main causes of nosebleeds are dry air (when your nasal membranes dry out, they're more susceptible to bleeding) a nose collision and nose picking. To keep the inside of your nose moist, use saline spray several times a day or try putting a thin layer of petroleum jelly in your nostrils with a cotton swab before bed. Noses bleed easily with a minor injury as well. Treatment is to gently pinch the nose closed, just below the nasal bones, and remain still until the bleed stops. Continue pinching for at least 10 minutes without stopping for best results. Do not blow the clot out to allow it to heal. Another method for difficult nosebleeds: Gently blow your nose to clear out the blood clots. Then spray both sides of your nose with a nasal decongestant like Afrin. Pinch your nose shut for 10 – 15 minutes without stopping. If bleeding continues, do another 10-15 minutes. If the bleeding is still perfuse, seek medical care. Excessive bleeding can also be a sign of a bleeding disorder or related to taking blood thinners. If so, contact your physician.

<u>Ear Ache:</u> Pain in the inner ear is most likely fluid pressure associated with allergies/colds/flu/sinus. Extreme pain and fever, especially in infants/children, may be bacterial and a doctor may prescribe an antibiotic. Otherwise, alternate hot and cold packs lying down with ear up. Warm colloidal silver drops or olive oil with garlic juice drops placed in the ear are worth trying. Chiropractic adjustment is sometimes helpful. Chew gum if the ear pain is related to altitude or airplane cabin pressure. Do not put anything in the ear if there is bleeding as this could indicate a ruptured eardrum or a trauma.

<u>Dental Pain:</u> Pain may be due to a tooth breaking through the gum (infant teething or wisdom teeth in teens). Gums can be irritated or infected which is seen as puffiness and/or bleeding. Dental nerve pain can be from an exposed nerve or root because of a cavity, cracked or broken tooth. Prevention is key – both daily teeth brushing and flossing, as well as not biting hard things like ice and popcorn kernels. A temporary filling can be made from the drug store kits (clove oil and zinc oxide powder). Clove oil may also provide some temporary pain relief. Jaw aches caused by infected, impacted or abscessed teeth requires dental care to prevent serious bone or sinus infections. Alternating heat/cold treatments may provide some short term relief.

<u>First aid for Eyes:</u> For chemical exposure (wash your hands quickly, if you wear contacts remove them!) Begin flushing immediately and continue for 15 minutes. Seek medical care. It may help your care provider if you can tell them what the chemical is, so take the bottle or label with you.

If you have a particle in your eye, don't rub your eye! Wash hands first and then try flushing the eye with water. Blink and see if tears will float it out. If you can see the object, you may try to remove it with a moistened q-tip or moist clean cloth. If it is stuck or embedded you will not be able to remove it and rubbing will only increase the damage. In this case a doctor will need to remove the particle; do not delay.

Pinkeye, also known as conjunctivitis, is a very contagious infection common in children. Pinkeye causes the white of the eye (sclera) to turn red, creates a yellow crust on eyelids or lashes, yellow or green discharge, eyes that burn or feel gritty, and light sensitivity. People are kept home from school and work and are treated with antibiotic eye drops.

Acute visual distress can result from detached retina or acute glaucoma. Symptoms include eye pain, headache, blurred vision, seeing halos, rainbows, flashes of light, large increase of "floaters" and nausea/vomiting. If the retina detaches it pulls away from the back of the eye creating a darkening "curtain" or shadow covering part of your vision. It is usually painless, but threatens the total loss of vision, so you will need immediate medical attention.

Appendix J: Mechanic Tools Lists

Hand tools and related items:

1. Measuring tools: tape, yard stick, speed square, carpenters square, line-level, levels, stud finder

2. Marking tools: carpenters pencil, permanent markers, chalk line

3. Stands (saw horses, jack stands)

4. Hammers (regular, small sledge, ball peen, rubber mallet), anvil

5. Grab tools: pliers (regular, needle nose – straight and bent nose), vice-grip, channel locks, locking pliers, adjustable wrenches, pipe wrench, multiple size wrenches in both standard and metric (box end wrenches, socket sets, extended sockets, hex wrenches)

6. Cutting tools: scissors, exacto knife, wood plane, wire cutters, wire strippers, wire snips, tin snips, bolt cutters, tap and dye set (making threads), cutting torch

7. Saws: hack-saw, coping saw, hole-saw

8. Manual drill and bits, nail punch, chisel

9. Fastening tools: c-clamps, quick grip, hose clamps, zip ties, pinch-grip clamps, pipe clamps, magnets, staple gun and staples, various fasteners (nuts, bolts, washers, lock washers, nails, screws, wire nuts, etc.), oxy-acetylene welder

 10. Screw drivers in various sizes: flat head, Phillips, star, etc.

12. Glues: superglue, Gorilla, wood, JB weld, epoxy, calk gun & calks

13. Tape: electrical, duct, plumbers

14. Filing/scraping tools: various wood and metal files, sand papers, steel wool, scruffy pads, scrapers

15. Brushes: tooth brush, Wisk broom, metal brushes, bristle

16. Cloth joining: rivet gun and rivets, chain rivet extractor, grommet setter set and grommets

17. Illumination: flood lamps and flashlights

18. Air insertion: manual air pump, pressure gauge

19. Pulling tools: crow bars, cats-paw (nail puller),

20. Ladders

<u>Power tools and battery power tools</u> (if I have power): *Air compressor *electric hand drills (drill bits) *drill press *wet/dry vacuum *power washer *lathe *table belt sander *hand held belt sander *orbital sander * table saw *chop saw *metal chop saw *hand held saws (circular, reciprocating, jig) *drimel tool and bits *soldering iron and solder *heat gun *table mount grinder *hand held grinder *welders.

Appendix K: Priest – List of Scripture Foundations

1. **What does the Bible say about itself?** 2 Timothy 3:16-17 - **"All Scripture is God-breathed and is useful for teaching, rebuking, correcting, and training in righteousness, so that the servant of God may be thoroughly equipped for every good work"**

2. **Who does God say that He is?** Isaiah 44:24 – **"Thus says the Lord, your Redeemer, And He who formed you from the womb: 'I am the Lord, who makes all things, Who stretches out the heavens all alone, Who spreads abroad the earth by Myself;'"**

3. **Who does the Bible say Jesus is?** John 1:1 **"In the beginning was the Word, and the Word was with God, and the Word was God."** John 1:14 **"The Word became flesh and made his dwelling among us. We have seen his glory, the glory of the one and only Son, who came from the Father, full of grace and truth."** Philippians 2:10-11 **"that at the name of Jesus every knee should bow, of those in heaven, and of those on earth, and of those under the earth, [11] and that every tongue should confess that Jesus Christ is Lord, to the glory of God the Father."**

4. **Who does the Bible say the Holy Spirit is?** John 14:16-17 **'And I will pray the Father, and He will give you another Helper, that He may abide with you forever— [17] the Spirit of truth, whom the world cannot receive, because it neither sees Him nor knows Him; but you know Him, for He dwells with you and will be in you.'**

5. **How is Jesus a priest and how can you then claim that priestly authority?** Hebrews 7:17 **"For He [God] testifies [of Jesus]: 'You are a priest forever According to the order of Melchizedek.' 1Peter 2:5 'you [Christians] also, as living**

stones, are being built up a spiritual house, a holy priesthood, to offer up spiritual sacrifices acceptable to God through Jesus Christ.'

6. Who is our needed mediator between us and the Lord? John 14:6 "Jesus said to him," 'I am the way, the truth, and the life. No one comes to the Father except through Me.' 1Tim 2:5-6 "For there is one God and one Mediator between God and men, the Man Christ Jesus, [6] who gave Himself a ransom for all, to be testified in due time,...".

7. How do we worship God? John 4:24 "God is Spirit, and those who worship Him must worship in spirit and truth." This is why an alternative religion will not reach God regardless of sincerity – you have to go with God's rules!

8. How do we know that we can trust God? Numbers 23:19 "God is not a man, that He should lie, Nor a son of man, that He should repent. Has He said, and will He not do? Or has He spoken, and will He not make it good?"

9. What blessing can you give to those in your spiritual care? Numbers 6:24-26 "The Lord bless you and keep you; [25] The Lord make His face shine upon you, And be gracious to you; [26] The Lord lift up His countenance upon you, And give you peace."

10. Is there really such a thing as a curse and if so how is it broken? Deuteronomy 10: 6-7 "Then the LORD passed in front of Moses and called out:" 'The LORD, the LORD God, is compassionate and gracious, slow to anger, abounding in loving devotion and faithfulness, 7 maintaining loving

devotion to a thousand generations, forgiving iniquity, transgression, and sin. Yet He will by no means leave the guilty unpunished; He will visit the iniquity of the fathers on their children and grandchildren to the third and fourth generations.' Galatians 3:13 "Christ redeemed us from the curse of the Law by becoming a curse for us. For it is written: 'Cursed is everyone who is hung on a tree [the cross].' Proverbs 26:2 "Like a flitting sparrow, like a flying swallow, So a curse without cause shall not alight." This means without legal grounds the curse of your enemies won't stick.

11. The marks of your spiritual maturity are shown by the demonstrated fruit of the Spirit in your life – Galations 5:22-23 "But the fruit of the Spirit is love, joy, peace, longsuffering, kindness, goodness, faithfulness, [23] gentleness, self-control. Against such there is no law."

12. What do you do with Mark 16:17-18 in these last days? "And these signs will follow those who believe: In My name they will cast out demons; they will speak with new tongues; [18] they will take up serpents (example of Paul gathering wood); and if they drink anything deadly, it will by no means hurt them; they will lay hands on the sick, and they will recover." This is actually a pretty tough one so you may want to read *Christ the Healer* by F.F. Bosworth (ISBN 978-0-8007-9457-6) and definitely the booklet by Kenneth Hagin called *Why Tongues* (ISBN 978-0-89276-051-0).

13. What do you know about the spiritual gifts for yourself and for the Christian believers in your Tribe? 1 Corinthians 4 -11: "There are diversities of gifts, but the same Spirit. [5] There are differences of ministries, but the same Lord. [6] And there are diversities of activities, but it is the same God who works all in all. [7] But the manifestation of the Spirit is given to each one for the profit of all: [8] for to one is given the word of wisdom through the Spirit, to another the word of knowledge through the same

Spirit, [9] to another faith by the same Spirit, to another gifts of healings by the same Spirit, [10] to another the working of miracles, to another prophecy, to another discerning of spirits, to another different kinds of tongues, to another the interpretation of tongues. [11] But one and the same Spirit works all these things, distributing to each one individually as He wills."

14.   You are living in a spiritual war zone (this may also manifest itself in the physical) and will need the full armor of God to stand firm. Ephesians 6: 11-18 "Put on the whole armor of God, that you may be able to stand against the wiles of the devil. [12] For we do not wrestle against flesh and blood, but against principalities, against powers, against the rulers of the darkness of this age, against spiritual hosts of wickedness in the heavenly places. [13] Therefore take up the whole armor of God, that you may be able to withstand in the evil day, and having done all, to stand. [14] Stand therefore, having girded your waist with truth, having put on the breastplate of righteousness (Jesus), [15] and having shod your feet with the preparation of the gospel of peace; [16] above all, taking the shield of faith with which you will be able to quench all the fiery darts of the wicked one. [17] And take the helmet of salvation, and the sword of the Spirit, which is the word of God; [18] praying always with all prayer and supplication in the Spirit, being watchful to this end with all perseverance and supplication for all the saints." This subject was thought to be so important to the early Puritans that William Gurnall wrote a three volume series called The Christian in Complete Armour (the abridged ISBN 978-0-85151-568-7).

15.   How can you practice the prayer that Jesus gave to His disciples – the Lord's Prayer (see Matthew 6:5-14)? Larry Lea's Could You Not Tarry One Hour? (ISBN9780884192107) uses this as a model to expand this prayer to: a) list eight names of God and their benefits to us; b) asking for God's will (yourself and family, church and pastor, nation-wide political and spiritual

leaders and for the harvest of souls); daily provision (being in God's will for our spiritual life, giving and our work habits); asking God to forgive us and help to forgive others; delivering us from evil (putting on our component armor and praying for a hedge of divine protection); declaring that His is the Kingdom, Power & Glory forever (finish by praising Him and making your faith declarations).

16.   What does the Bible say about forgiveness? Ephesians 4:32 says "And be kind to one another, tenderhearted, forgiving one another, even as God in Christ forgave you." Proverbs 28:13 – "He who covers his sins will not prosper, But whoever confesses and forsakes *them* will have mercy." Mark 11:25 – "And whenever you stand praying, if you have anything against anyone, forgive him, that your Father in heaven may also forgive you your trespasses." (Personally, I find the hardest person to forgive is myself)! Learn to show compassion to yourself – guilt implies that you are a good person (Christ's righteousness), who nevertheless did something bad vs. shame (you see yourself as a bad person).

17.   2 Timothy 4:2&5 admonishes you to: "Preach the word (Bible)! Be ready in season and out of season. Convince, rebuke, exhort, with all longsuffering and teaching. 5 But you be watchful in all things, endure afflictions, do the work of an evangelist, fulfill your ministry."

This may seem like an overwhelming list, but even priests have to start somewhere. If this is your heart's desire - it pleases God and know that Christ will help you attain it. Hebrews 12:2 "looking unto Jesus, the author and finisher of *our* faith, who for the joy that was set before Him endured the cross, despising the shame, and has sat down at the right hand of the throne of God." As a matter of fact, in 2 Corinthians 12:9 the Apostle Paul recorded these words – "And He (Jesus) said to me, "My grace is sufficient for you, for My strength is made perfect in weakness.

Appendix L: Preparedness – One Page Summary

Prov. 22:3 **"A Prudent man sees danger and takes refuge**, but the simple keeps going and suffers for it." 1 Cor. 14:12 "weigh carefully (judge) what is said…"

Individually, for an extended disaster/crisis, it makes sense to prepare in these areas:

1) **Gear** – flashlight, candle/matches, clothing, rain gear, work gloves, tools, meds, duct tape, first-aid kit, sleep bag, bug spray, cook stuff, shelter, Bible, this book
2) **Grub** – food and water (you determine: gov't. says 3-days; weeks/months?)
3) **Green backs** (Gold or barter) – buy/trade for essentials that eventually run out
4) **Guard-dog** (Guns & ammo; pepper spray?) – security or protection if necessary
5) **God -relationship** for faith vs. fear; _Jesus benefit link_ (Psalm 91:14-16) "The angel of the Lord encamps around those who reverence Him, …" Ps. 34:7

"Tribes" are small groups of people who come together for mutual help and synergy*. (*The Clydesdale analogy – one horse can pull 7,000 pounds, but two can pull 18,000 pounds; however if they are properly matched and trained they can pull 25,000 pounds). **Communities** - friendly groups of "tribes" in a geographic area provide additional depth. _Ecc. 4:12 "Though one may be overpowered, two can defend themselves. A cord of three strands is not quickly broken." Heb. 10:25, "Let us not give up meeting together…_

Functions needed within a **"tribe"** in a longer term crisis would include the following:

1) **Master-Gardener** (grow/harvest food, weed, preserve food, save seed, animals)
   Prov. 28:19 "He who works his land will have abundant food…"; Gen 1:29, 2:15
2) **Medical** (first-aid, medical care, sanitation/disease prevention, natural health)
   Luke 10:33-34 (Story of the Good Samaritan who took pity and bandaged wounds)
3) **Mechanic** (maintenance, fabricator, carpenter and other trade skills, engineer)
   Exodus 36:1 "…every skilled person to whom the Lord has given skill and ability…"
   Prov. 8:12 "I wisdom dwell with prudence, & find out knowledge of witty inventions"
4) **Merchant** (barterer, scrounger, entrepreneur, capitalist – present income or savings)
   Prov. 31:16-20 (Woman who buys a field, plants a vineyard, makes/trades profitably)
5) **Protector** (warrior, concealment, communications, hunt/fish/trap, energy and water)
   Ps. 18:34-35 "He trains my hands for battle…" "You give me your shield of victory…"
   Hebrews 12:4 Make every effort to live in peace with all men…"
6) **Provisioner** (quartermaster, gatherer, cook, wash/sew, library, teach/care of young)
   Prov. 31:13-15 (Skilled woman who provides food, clothing & other domestic needs)
7) **Priest** (spiritual gifts and spiritual warfare, teacher, encourager, counselor, mediator)
   1 Cor. 12:1 "To one there is given through the Spirit the message of wisdom, to another the message of knowledge…" 1Peter 2:9 "But you are a chosen people, a royal priesthood…" 2Cor.10:4 "The weapons we fight with…. have divine power…"
8) **Pre-crisis job skills** (other job skills or income sources in this season of crisis).

Appendix M: 12 Reasons NOT to Prepare for Hard Times
Answer True or False to each question:

T/F God knows that I am too busy to prepare – so He will <u>supernaturally</u> provide for me

Hints: "by faith Noah built…"; Joseph's stores; no Christians present at Jerusalem fall

T/F I wouldn't know how to prepare so it's just better to not think about it

Hints: Seek out those who do know; library books; internet, read this entire book!

T/F I don't have money for preparations or I don't want to waste money for no reason

Hints: Many preps are low cost; think of it as insurance; buy what you use & use it

T/F I'll get my preparations when and if a catastrophe actually happens

Hints: Can you get insurance after an accident; store shelves are bare in 3 days

T/F I live in America, so it is FEMA's job (or charities) to feed and house me

Hints: Houston Astrodome Katrina debacle; 1950's gov't. stockpiles no longer exist

T/F Even if I did prepare, someone would just steal it

Hint: Do you have the God given right of self defense; will you have limited charity?

T/F I plan to just head to the mountains to survive by hunting and fishing

Hints: Are you really that skilled; How many people have the same idea (crowding)?

T/F I will just head out to the countryside where surplus food is free and abundant

Hints: Farmers are 2% of the US population and they grocery shop at Wal-Mart too

T/F I can always grow a garden, raise all my own food and chop wood for heat

Hints: Is this garden started; do you know how to can; where are these dead trees?

T/F My extended family is already prepared and they will take care of me

Hint: Verify both statements immediately and see what they need <u>you</u> to contribute now

T/F My neighbors and friends will take care of me

Hints: Find out if they are prepared themselves and have all extra preparations for you

T/F My church has the resources to physically provide for me and my entire family

Hints: Confirm this with your Pastor; is God your Jehovah-Jireh? - churches are not!

<u>Help yourself</u> with the one page Preparedness Summary (Appendix L)

Do it NOW without delay - preparation is the action of Faith!